Xs, Os, and Ws

Inspirational Stories
From Successful Basketball Coaches

C. Nathaniel Brown

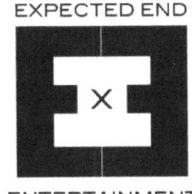

Atlanta, GA

Copyright © 2014 C. Nathaniel Brown
All rights reserved. No part of this book may be reproduced or transmitted in any form or by any means, electronic or mechanical, including photocopy, recording, or by any information storage and retrieval system with the exception of a reviewer who may quote brief passages in a review to be printed in a blog, newspaper or magazine without written permission from the author. Address inquiries to: Expected End Entertainment, P.O. Box 1751, Mableton, GA 30126.
Published by Expected End Entertainment/EX3 Books
ExpectedEndEntertainment@gmail.com
ISBN-10: 0988554542
ISBN-13: 978-0-9885545-4-2
Printed in the United States of America

This book is dedicated to the men and women who have accepted the call to teach, coach, and impact others utilizing the game of basketball. Thank you to the players who allowed me to be their coach. You will always be my sons and daughters.

Contents

FOREWORD 13
    Jemele Hill, ESPN Sports Journalist............................. 13
INTRODUCTION 17
A CULTURE OF SUCCESS 21
    PAT SUMMIT 21
COACHING 'PISTOL' PETE MARAVICH............................ 23
    GREG BERNBROCK... 23
BLACK BLAZER AND TIGERS PATCH 27
    TERRY STOTTS 27
A TEAM PLAYER 29
    MORGAN WOOTEN 29
BALANCING FUN, COACHING YOUR SONS, AND LEBRON JAMES 35
    DRU JOYCE II 35
BEFORE YOU CAN TEACH, YOU GOT TO REACH 39
    GANON BAKER.. 39
COMPLACENCY CAN GET YOU REPLACED 43
    SHARMAN WHITE.. 43
THE MAKING OF A NAME 47
    LUTE OLSON 47
A SHOT OF CHARACTER 53

HOMER DREW	53
MAKING THE BEST 'WE' WE CAN	57
SCOTT DREW	57
RESPECT WITHOUT FEAR	61
FRED WILLIAMS	61
RECIPE FOR SUCCESS	65
STEVE SMITH	65
MY MOM WAS MY BEST COACH	69
VINCE TAYLOR	69
PHENOMENAL WOMEN	73
ADELL HARRIS	73
WE ARE INDEED FAMILY	77
CABRAL HUFF	77
THERE HAS TO BE BALANCE	81
DARRYL SHARP	81
JUST A GOD THING	85
JAMES NAKAMURA	85
NO FEAR, NO DOUBT	89
MIKE DAVIS	89
COACH JESUS, TEAM DISCIPLES	93
ALLEN RAY	93
HOME SWEET HOME	97

TOM BOSLEY	97
IT'S ALL COMING TOGETHER	101
DARYL HOUSE	101
SELFLESS, EDUCATED MEN OF CHARACTER AND ACTION	105
BOB GHILONI	105
COACHING IS LIKE MANAGING	109
LONNIE BARTLEY	109
YOU HAVE WHAT IT TAKES	113
YOLANDA MOORE	113
THE SWOT TEAM	117
GEORGE ELLIS	117
BUILT FOR BLUE COLLAR WORK	121
BEN HOWLAND	121
MOTIVATED TO DO THIS	125
DON PITTMAN	125
DUMB LUCK	129
CARL ARRIGALE	129
BORN TO COACH	133
TRACY DILDY	133
VALUE SUCCESS ON THE IMPACT	137
STEPHANIE WHITE	137

SHOOTING UNDER THE MOONLIGHT	143
CORY ARNETT	143
THE HARDER YOU WORK, THE LUCKIER YOU GET	145
LEFTY DRIESELL	145
LEGACY BUILDS SUCCESS	147
JOEL HAWKINS	147
FAMILY AND SUCCESS GO HAND IN HAND	151
RICK INSELL	151
WINDOW INTO THE WORLD	155
POKEY CHATMAN	155
STAND FOR SOMETHING	159
MIKE KAYES	159
PARENTING A PROGRAM	163
RAY LOKAR	163
BIG GAME PHILOSOPHY	167
PETE POMPEY	167
LOVE, RESPECT AND EDUCATION	173
RON 'FANG' MITCHELL	173
MY DOOR IS ALWAYS OPEN	177
DICK BENNETT	177
BUILDING TEAMWORK	181
JAMES KAHN	181

THE IMPORTANCE OF SYSTEM	185
SHANE DREILING	185
86,400 SECONDS	189
LARRY MCKENZIE	189
IT'S FOR THE BIG PICTURE	193
MICHAEL COOPER	193
WE ALL GROW	197
BOB HUGGINS	197
'FAMILY' IS NO CLICHÉ HERE	199
ALAN HUSS	199
RELATIONSHIPS, LEARNING AND SUCCESS	203
ANNE DONOVAN	203
ALL ABOUT THE ABC'S	207
PATRICK WALTON	207
OUT OF YOURSELF	211
AND INTO THE TEAM	211
SARA LEE	211
OUTWORK THE NEXT PERSON	215
TERRY PORTER	215
MIND CANDY AND COMMUNICATION	217
DON SHOWALTER	217
CARRYING THE TRADITION	221

- DIEGO JONES 221
- SOMETHING'S GOING TO HAPPEN 223
  - RYAN HUMPHREY 223
- SPORTS TEACH LIFE LESSONS 227
  - DWAYNE CHERRY 227
- IT HAS TO START WITH ME 231
  - MIKE JONES 231
- THE DEMATHA OF THE MIDWEST 235
  - KYLE LINDSTED 235
- SPORTS IS AN EQUALIZER 239
  - BET NAUMOVSKI 239
- THE 3 C'S: THE COURT, THE CLASSROOM AND THE COMMUNITY 243
  - JILL PRUDDEN 243
- WE WILL ALWAYS BE FAMILY 245
  - SCOTTIE RICHARDSON 245
- WE NEED TO BE THE BEST LEARNERS 247
  - PATRICK RUFENER 247
- BE A TRANSFORMATIONAL COACH 251
  - LASON PERKINS 251
- BUILD CHARACTER 253
  - DON RUEDLINGER 253

ALL IN	255
PAT SULLIVAN	255
USE BASKETBALL AS A VEHICLE	257
SCOONIE PENN	257
QUOTES	261
OTHER FAMOUS QUOTES	265
AFTERWORDS	269
ABOUT THE AUTHOR	271

FOREWORD
Jemele Hill, ESPN Sports Journalist
Co-Host of Numbers Never Lie

I was the classic tomboy. I hated dresses. I didn't like dolls. I didn't wear earrings. I thought makeup was gross.

I didn't like anything that other girls my age did. But I loved activity. I loved competition. I loved physical challenges. It was pretty clear that I loved sports far more than I would ever love Barbie.

I was the lone girl hanging with the fellas when they wanted to do backflips off garages onto mattresses. I was the one girl they let play kickball, baseball, two square (it's a Detroit thing), basketball, or freeze tag. I felt like I was granted access into an exclusive club. The boys in my neighborhood and those I went to school with were my first coaches. They taught me how to compete, how to develop thick skin, and how to craft a pretty good insult. They didn't take it easy on me.

They eventually accepted me because it was pretty hard to argue girls weren't good at sports when I was playing quarterback on the neighborhood pickup football team (running my own version of Notre Dame's option-quarterback offense) and when we played baseball, I was throwing fools out from deep in the outfield.

As I progressed as an athlete, those early playground battles would be the foundation for how I developed a relationship with every coach that ever coached me. And for that matter, every manager that supervised me as a professional sports journalist. Other than the boys in my neighborhood, the coaches who influenced me the most were my fast-pitch softball coaches, Coach Fe – short for Felicia – and Coach Bowie. Although they had different personalities, they shared and preached the same values – values that

I adopted and used as guiding principles throughout my life.

They were both smart, fair and passionate. I always was among the best players on all of my teams, but neither Coach Fe nor Coach Bowie ever let me cut corners. I played for Coach Bowie for three years at Mumford High School. I still remember the day I tried out for the team. I was a little cocky, and boastfully told Coach Bowie I had been playing my whole life.

She nodded, and called a girl named Carla, who was much bigger than me and had one of the meanest glares I'd ever seen, to throw with me. My cockiness quickly left and I was suddenly a little intimidated. After one throw, it was clear that Carla had a ridiculous arm. Her first throw stung my hand, but I caught it and returned some heat of my own. I wasn't going to let her punk me! The entire time Carla and I threw, Coach Bowie stood there and watched. She didn't act impressed, even though it was obvious that I was one of the best girls at the tryout.

I was ecstatic and relieved when Coach Bowie told me I made the team. But she made it known that despite giving me a starting spot right away she was going to treat me like every other rookie. Over the next few years, Coach Bowie and I developed a close bond. She never changed, and when I became a captain, she held me to an even higher standard as a leader.

My dynamic with Coach Fe was different. I played for her primarily in the summer. She put together a team that was loaded with some of the best players in the city, and we competed in tournaments all over the state. I was a captain and either the best or second-best player on my high school team. But on Coach Fe's teams, I was perhaps the eighth or ninth-best player. I was low on the totem pole and for the first time in my athletic career, a benchwarmer. Without having to tell her, Coach Fe knew that my confidence was shaky. She practiced more love, than tough love.

Even if I made a routine play, she would make sure to give me a pat on the shoulder or tell me I did a good job. If I messed up, she would pull me aside and either show me how I could have made the play or explain to me how I made a poor decision.

That, to me, is great coaching. Athletes have a lot of pride and a lot of times, they are reluctant to verbalize weaknesses. I didn't have to tell Coach Fe how I felt in order for her to coach and develop me. It was the same with Coach Bowie. She knew that I could fall victim to complacency. She taught me how to be a leader and an example for others. It truly made me understand the biblical proverb, "To whom much is given, much is expected."

Like the majority of high school athletes, my athletic career ended when I graduated from high school, even though my love for sports did not. The lessons I learned from my coaches, Coach Fe and Coach Bowie, and the boys I grew up, are a big reason I've been able to thrive in the male-dominated industry of sports media.

I'll never embrace girly-girl things, but thanks to these influences, I'll always love challenges and maximize my potential.

INTRODUCTION

I wanted to be one of the success stories that looked back and attributed a portion of my success to the coaches that taught me character, what real success meant, and how to translate the game of sports to the game of life. But my youth coaches were not the most upstanding or professional people you would ever meet. My high school baseball coach was good for what he did and I've never forgotten the stories and memories that came along with that experience. But it wasn't the life-changing, impactful speech that I can reflect back to and say, "That was the moment the light came on!" I thought I would get it when I played basketball for the best high school in the country, Paul Laurence Dunbar High School in Baltimore, Maryland, where at the time Bob Wade coached and then turned the reigns over to Pete Pompey. But a funny thing happened. I never got the chance to play for either of them. The closest I got was a week's worth of open gym before tryouts and overhearing them talk to others about Xs and Os and life.

I had been a huge basketball fan, following my favorite teams, like the Los Angeles Lakers and Georgetown Hoyas; my favorite players like Nate 'Tiny' Archibald, Magic Johnson and Isiah Thomas; and studying the legends of the game. I loved playing the game every opportunity I got. I loved developing my skills, trying to add components to match some of the greats like the ball handling and passing skills of 'Pistol' Pete Maravich and the shooting touch of Jerry West and Larry Bird. I wanted to add flair like Dr. J, George Gervin and Dominique Wilkins, but that was limited since at 5'6-5'7 I was a little height challenged. My success came below the rim being able to score and distribute the ball, much like Archibald.

I felt like a fish out of water at open gym. It seemed like everybody else in the gym at Dunbar knew one another, played together, or had already been on the team so they played well together. Like me, they had dreams of being the next great basketball player to star at Dunbar, which produced arguably the best high school basketball team ever in the early 1980s that produced three first round NBA draft picks in Muggsy Bogues, Reggie Williams, and Reggie Lewis. But they had some things I didn't... friends on the court, more experience, and might I add... more talent (some of them). My claim to fame during that week of open gym is briefly playing with Sam Cassell, who went on to win three NBA championships, and leading a dream fast break and throwing an alley-oop to Hensley Parks, one of the humblest people I ever met. I cherish those memories, all of my memories at Dunbar.

Being unable to play for Dunbar did something I could not have imagined at the time. I went from being a basketball loving fan to a ridiculously fanatic basketball fan. I watched the games from the stands and dissected plays. I learned more about the rules of the game. I studied the preparation for games, scouting, and designing plays. I was slowly becoming a coach in the stands, sometimes a disgruntled one when the coaches wouldn't do what I thought they should do.

When I went to college, it continued. My passion quickly got under the skin of the coach because it sounded more like heckling than suggestions. I channeled that energy into intramurals and even becoming a certified official for Ohio high school basketball.

But it wasn't until my son was old enough to play in the YMCA basketball league that I finally got to put my knowledge to the test as a coach. You would've thought the Lakers had just signed me to coach the Magic Johnson-led championship team. I was serious! I was focused! I was game planning! I was scouting! I had whistles and whiteboards. I was ready. I got to the gym and realized... these kids don't know the rules of the game, how to dribble, how to shoot, how to play defense or anything. My job was to teach them. I quickly learned that I had to instill in them principles that would help them with the game of basketball but also help build a foundation for later in life.

I carried that mindset along as I got more invested in the kids. I eventually helped someone coach an AAU team one summer and the next year fielded my own team in Pittsburgh. I assembled some of the best players in the city and set out to teach them about basketball and life and present to them experiences and opportunities they hadn't had at that point. One summer, I had the opportunity to take the team to Ohio, about a two-hour drive, for a single elimination tournament. We lost our first game and as we sat in the hotel room, a couple of the players wanted to return to Pittsburgh that night. But one of the players stood up, repeated some words that I shared earlier about what being a team is, about building character, and about learning lessons from good and bad experiences.

See, only one member of the team of the team had traveled outside of the City of Pittsburgh before. So we utilized that opportunity to watch better teams and players, tour the area and bond. I learned a lot from that group of young men and I realized that if I continued to pour into them, one day it would come back to their remembrance and maybe, just maybe, it would help them live productive lives and have positive impacts on their communities.

At that same time, I began studying other coaches who had successful basketball coaching careers as well as positive impacts on their players. I attended coaching clinics with the likes of Mark Few, Tom Izzo, Bill Self, and Billy Donovan. I studied legendary coaches like John Wooden, Red Auerbach, Pat Riley, and Dean Smith. I listened to the stories that players such as Bill Russell, Grant Hill, Michael Jordan, and others shared about the impact that their coaches had on them in basketball and life. They talked about success, wisdom, character, faith, and family. The more I read and watched, the more I wanted to reach out to other coaches to hear their stories.

So as I coached AAU teams and later high school boys and girls at Greater Works Academy, a private Christian school just outside of Pittsburgh, I took every opportunity to interview coaches on all levels. Some I sat down with at coaching clinics. I met others at their offices. And some we spoke over the phone. Coaches would return my calls while I was at work as a newspaper reporter and I would sneak away to the conference room to interview them. I began forming the framework for Xs, Os, and Ws: Inspirational Stories from Successful Basketball Coaches. I wanted to be inspired and motivated but I also wanted to share the stories with others. After several years passed, I picked up the stories and was inspired and motivated to finish the project. I know that many basketball players and coaches will also find these stories refreshing. Maybe there will be something that you read that one day you will share with someone else. There is plenty of inspiration to go around.

C. Nathaniel Brown
"Chuck"

A CULTURE OF SUCCESS
PAT SUMMIT

There is no greater feeling than having a young lady come to me and say, 'Hey Coach, I appreciate what you did for me. I appreciate you for believing in me and teaching me how to be successful."

I've always had a passion for the game of basketball. But I learned early on in my coaching career that basketball could be used as a tool to develop leaders and prepare young women for life. Some people don't realize it but basketball is a privilege. It's not a right. So I've utilized this platform to teach my players how to take advantage of the opportunities that are set before them, to get their education, to grow into the best women they can be, become the best basketball players they can be.

We've been successful because we've had some outstanding young women come through the University of Tennessee. They entrusted me to teach them about the game of basketball and life. But what they didn't know is that they would teach me a thing or two over the years as well. I've grown as a coach and as a person because of the people who have been a part of this program. I love every single one of them.

Because we've been successful over the years, people think it's been easy. But they don't see all of the hard work that these young women put in every day. They don't see the staff's work to put these young women in the best possible situations to be successful. And because we've been successful, we have to make sure that we don't get complacent. None of us like to lose. But not all of them are accustomed to the hard work it takes to maintain success. But they learn. It's a part of the maturation process and growing into who you are supposed to be. Success is about hard work and learning along the way.

I often tell them that every moment is a teaching moment. My players will tell you that I will stop them in the middle of a sentence, or stop them in the middle of a play, or just see them around campus, and I will share with them something I think will help them. Most of the time, it has nothing to do with basketball. I've coached some smart players. Some of them were naturally gifted and could easily pick up the things we implemented on the court. But I'm just as concerned with them outside and beyond basketball, in the classroom, in their families, in their social life.

That's why we recruit players with character who are leaders or who desire to become leaders. We want to create a culture of success for them and teach them how to create a culture of success for themselves once they graduate. I think we've done pretty well so far.

Pat Summit won eight NCAA championships, 16 SEC championships, and appeared in 17 Final Fours as head women's coach at the University of Tennessee from 1974-2012. She currently serves as coach emeritus. Summit was inducted in the Basketball Hall of Fame in 2000 and was named Naismith Basketball coach of the century the same year. She is the winningest coach in college basketball history.

COACHING 'PISTOL' PETE MARAVICH
GREG BERNBROCK

There are so many memories as it relates not just to Pete but our team. There are certain records in sports that are pretty much untouchable. I'm sitting here looking at a lot of Coach John Wooden's philosophy who we were close to back then. Obviously there are other great coaches too. But I remember when we went to what was then called the Rainbow Classic out in Honolulu. It was December of 1970. We were playing in the championship and we beat St. John's, who always a powerhouse out of New York. Pete was leading the country in scoring. But there were two other prolific scorers, Rick Mount at Purdue, and Calvin Murphy at Niagara. All three of those guys were in the 40s. All were just terrific ball players.

They decided to not guard Pete. They decided they were going to play a Box and 1 and just leave him open. It was unbelievable. It took Pete almost a half to get used to not being guarded because he was accustomed to not just having one person but two or three on him. They just let him alone. True to form, he would hit the open man. I don't remember the score but they were up at half. They were all fired up. They thought they had found the formula to stop Pete. They just left him alone.

So we went in at half and regrouped. Once he got his rhythm, the defense didn't work well the second half. I think he burned them for 30-35 points in the second half. It was funny because Lou Carnesecca still laughs at that. He said, 'At least we held him for a half.' It was something that took him by surprise, something totally unexpected. It took him a minute to figure it out but when he did, he was Pete.

He holds a lot of records. I doubt that his total points record would ever be eclipsed. Back then, there was no one and done. He played three varsity years. We also projected pretty accurately that if there had been a 3-point line, instead of averaging 44 points a game it would have added 3, 4, 5, shots a game. He took an awful lot of shots from the perimeter. We will never really know but it's feasible that he could have averaged 50 points a game.

We were at Oregon State one night and I don't know why they had this strategy but they kept fouling Pete. You didn't want to do that because he was a very, very accurate free throw shooter. So we're playing in an old barn. It was packed, probably 14,000-15,000 people in it. For some unknown reason they just continued to foul him. The bottom line is he shot 31 free throws. He missed 1. It's doubtful that will ever happen again. That's a Joe Dimaggio type record when he hit in 56 straight games. That's very unlikely that anybody's ever going to do that again. I'm not saying it can't happen but those are records that will probably stand the test of time.

It was one of those magical situations coaching a player like that. You just have to feel fortunate when it happens. I used to get asked, 'How do you coach Pete?' I'd say, 'I tell you right now, I just coach his left hand.' He was just an incredibly gifted athlete.

You have to give players the latitude to perform. You don't want to over coach. Or like we say in the business world, you don't want to over manage people. Micromanagement, generally speaking, is not very successful. The key is tremendous conditioning because you gotta be able to go. The next thing is discipline. Basketball players have an innate built in just like business people. They don't deviate from that. I know as a player myself and as a coach, it was always about the task at hand. You're shooting for goals, you set the goals as high as you can, and then you do everything you can not only to attain them but to repeat. So that was our philosophy. You set high goals, you exceed those goals and then you repeat.

Greg Bernbrock was an assistant coach of the LSU men's basketball team from 1964-1972. He served under Press Maravich and Jay McCreary and was an instrumental contributor in the development of 'Pistol' Pete Maravich.

BLACK BLAZER AND TIGERS PATCH
TERRY STOTTS

My dad was a high school basketball coach and I remember going to his practices when I was 5-6 years old and watching those practices and going on road trips when I was in elementary school. He was coaching Marshfield, Wisconsin, the Marshfield Tigers, and I would travel with the team with my little black blazer and a Tigers patch. I was always around the game because of my dad and I've just always been in love with the game.

As you're young and a player, for me anyway, I just loved being around the game. When I was in college, I worked basketball camps, working with junior high and high school kids. I enjoyed teaching them, watching them play and compete. That was my first taste of being around younger people and having them kind of look up to me or listening to what I was saying.

I didn't know where my career was going to go in basketball. But when I came out of high school and went to college, I majored in zoology, which is a science. If I did not have a career playing basketball, I was accepted into dental school and had planned to go to dental school after my undergraduate years.

When you look at success, it's developed over time. I've had a lot of people who have had an impact on my life. My father was certainly first and foremost, as far as who I am and striving to be a successful person whether it was in school, wanting to be a dentist or wanting to be the best basketball player I could be. That was all instilled by my parents but particularly my father.

At the NBA level, I think we choose players with high character. By the time they get here, they are who they are, as far as character because of their parents or coaches or their family members or significant others. I don't know how much at this stage that I influence their character but what we try to do is teach them to be professional, be on time, be respectful of teammates, to understand how important it is to do the right things with your job, and to know that you want to get better and be willing to work. They have habits but their character is pretty much intact. Teaching them to be a good pro and building good habits at the professional level is important to us.

Terry Stotts is the head basketball coach for the Portland Trailblazers. He began his coaching career as an assistant with George Karl and later became head coach of the Atlanta Hawks and Milwaukee Bucks. He won an NBA championship as an assistant with the Dallas Mavericks in 2011.

A TEAM PLAYER
MORGAN WOOTEN

My first real taste of success is when I tried out for the basketball team at Montgomery Blair High School when I was a sophomore in high school. I made the team. Actually, that was the first time that I tried out for a team and made it. I had played basketball for teams that you didn't have to try out for, you just automatically made them by showing up.

Here, I had to go out and compete and survive the cut list posting. I felt like I had become successful. I worked pretty hard to become a decent basketball player. The fact that I actually tried out and made the team, in the face of what all felt was great competition, really made me feel that I had achieved something grand.

I learned a lot from that experience. I think it was the beginning of my real love affair with basketball. I found out that with hard work you can achieve certain things.

I also made up in my mind that it seemed so cold to post a cut list. Anyone not on that list had to come to the reality that they had been cut. I didn't like that part of it. It stayed with me all of those years. Once I became a coach, I never posted a cut list. When I'm ready to let eight or nine kids go, after practice I'd call them in personally, one on one, sit down with them, talk about their future, their plans, try to ease the letdown, try to show them there are a lot more options available.

One year at Damatha, I'm working with the team and we're having tryouts. There was a young fellow that was a junior that I just didn't feel was going to make the team. I called him in, sat him down and I talked to him. I explained to him that it's not at all over, that if he went out and played Boys Club this year and work on his weaknesses and maybe play a little CYO, he could come back and try out for the team next year as a senior. That kid came back the next year and made the team. He was instrumental in us winning the championship. He had many a great ball games. He went to Gettysburg College on a full basketball scholarship and later went on to be a head coach, Perry Clark.

That goes way back to me seeing that first cut list posted. I said, 'Later, when I become a coach, I'm not going to do that.' And it sure paid off in Perry Clark and what a great example of character that was.

I also had a young guy that made varsity as a junior but didn't play a lot that year. He was very good and very valuable in practice but he had a lot of seniors sitting in front of him. I knew him well. He had been coming to my camps since he was seven years old. I knew his parents, his family. In fact, his mother had been an Olympic swimmer.

He said, "Coach, is DeMatha the right spot for me?" I said, 'Yeah, it's the right spot, son. This is the place for you.' As a senior, he was a pivotal piece in our basketball team and helped us with the championship. Today, that's Mike Brey, head coach at Notre Dame.

You're thrilled to see them be successful in any walk of life. That's the greatest thrill of coaching. I can remember my first year at DeMatha. I went up to New York City with Ernie Cage, one of my real good players, who was being recruited by St. John's University. The coach, Joe Lapchik, and I were at lunch and he said, "Let me tell you something coach. I know you are just getting started in your first year. But I want to tell you what coaching is all about. The greatest reward in coaching, 10-15 years later, is when a kid comes back with a big smile on his face and says, 'Hi Coach.' That's what coaching is all about. And if they're successful, that will mean everything."

Today, I don't care if they made it as a coach, a player or just a great human being. They're doing a good job. They're good family men. They're good American citizens. That's all you really hope for. Obviously, I get just as big a thrill out of a guy like James Brown, who was an All-American for me, but there are guys who went on to be doctors, lawyers, high school principals, electricians, solid family guys. It doesn't matter what the field is, I just like to see them do well. That's the greatest thrill of coaching.

Each senior at DeMatha fills out an exit questionnaire that talks about the principal and teachers that had an impact on their lives. A couple kids that never made the team have through the years put down on their exit slips that they learned a lot from me. Life is tough. It's not always fair. You don't always get what you think you deserve and you think that it will break your heart if you don't. But we learned out of disappointment, out of adversity comes strength. They talked about how they became stronger people through not making the team. So even if a guy doesn't make the team, you can still teach him a lot. It is through adversity that we gain strength and wisdom. I really stress that to a guy that doesn't make it.

I played one year at Montgomery Junior College and that was about as far as I could go as a player. Then they took the ball away from me and said I wasn't good enough to play any further past that, except sandlot leagues and things like that. The irony was I thought I was going to be a lawyer. I started Montgomery College in liberal arts and was going to go into pre-law. I also played football, basketball, and I boxed at Montgomery College. My uncle who worked for the Boys Club in Washington, called me up and said, "Morgan, St. Joe's Orphanage needs a baseball coach." I never played baseball. I was never any good at it at all. I said, "Let's try my friend Tony Clark." I talked to Tony and he said, "Maybe I'll take a crack at it. Take me over to see him." I took him over there to see the nun and when we got over there, Tommy started squirming. You could tell he didn't want the job. He started telling the nun, "Morgan's a candidate, too." The next thing I know I became a baseball coach. I never applied for the job.

I went over there and coached the baseball team and we went 0-166. The kids all said come back, we're better at football. We're tough. So by that point I fell in love with kids. I said, "These kids are great. They try so hard. They kept coming up empty but they really tried hard."

I went back and coached football and we went undefeated and I coached basketball and we had a good year. I think we finished in fourth place. I just became hooked on it and I changed my major to education.

You never know the direction the good Lord will point you in. My kids know about this story. I think they are intrigued by it. I've had some of them come back and say they thought they were headed in one direction and ended up somewhere else. But everything turned out okay.

I think it is human nature that any kid that's a pretty good high school player dreams of going to the NBA. They'll talk about it. I tell them to dream great dreams. Shoot for the stars and shoot for the moon. But while you're doing it, make sure you have a back-up plan. Make sure you're getting your education. Make sure you're prepared when they take that ball away from you.

Even if you do go to the NBA, they're going to take that ball away from you one day. Even if you play in the NBA for 10 years, you have two-thirds of your life to live when they take that ball away. You want to enjoy life. So I'm really preparing them for life after basketball whether that's when they leave DeMatha or if it's when they're done playing somewhere else.

I don't discourage the dream or the effort. I think that's wonderful. But they have to bring everything else along with them on the way. That's why I feel pretty good that 100 percent of my students have all begun college, 98 percent have graduated. So you feel pretty good about that.

Adrian Dantley, for example, graduated cap and gown from Notre Dame. Danny Ferry graduated from Duke University. James Brown is a Harvard graduate. Kenny Carr graduated from N.C. State and the list goes on. Some guys left college early and went back to get their degrees. Dantley left after his third year but went back and got his degree.

The paradox of coaching is that you want the individual to be the most fantastic individual they can become, the best players they can be, to be as good as they can get. Then you ask them all to sacrifice for the good of the team. It's a real delicate balancing act. Everyone remembers the great team but they don't always remember the great players that play on lousy teams. For years, the knock on Wilt Chamberlain was that he never had a ring. But Bill Russell had 11 or 12 of them. My question to them is do you want to be a great player that never won anything or do you want to be a very good player that played on a great team?

The DeMath-Power Memorial game is a good example. I tell my guys, "You probably can't name one guy on that DeMatha team. You can't tell me who the leading scorer in that game was. But it's history that DeMatha beat Lew Alcindor, later to become Kareem Abdul-Jabaar, gave him his only high school lost. That's always been the Power-Memorial team. The Power Team. The team that beat Power. People remember great teams."

The reason I experienced a level of success is because I was a pretty good player on a great team called DeMatha.

Morgan Wooten retired in 2002 as the winningest coach in boys and men's basketball history with 1,274 career victories and only 192 defeats. He led

DeMatha High School in Hyattsville, Maryland, to five national championships and 22 first place finishes in the Washington, D.C., metropolitan area in 46 years as its coach.

BALANCING FUN, COACHING YOUR SONS, AND LEBRON JAMES
DRU JOYCE II

I believe that you can do so much more with people you trust and enjoy being with. In today's world of athletics it's becoming harder and harder to accomplish that because people don't always view a team sport as a team sport anymore. They kind of view it as themselves and then some necessary guys in order to complete out a roster or the number of individuals on the playing field with them. There are a lot of guys who are great individual players but they're not good team players. What we've tried to do, and we've had varying degrees of success with it, is to try to take those 15 individuals and try to make them understand they are playing for something greater than themselves. We try to teach them that they are trying to accomplish something that is beyond their individual reach but working with their teammates, trusting their teammates, they can accomplish a lot of goals. And we allow them to have fun doing it.

I think if you're not having fun and it can't be fun, then I have to stop doing this. I know that sometimes we get so caught up in the winning and the losing that we lose sight of what coaching is about. Coaching is about teaching. It's not about just teaching the skills associated with the sport. It's about teaching those life lessons that arrive during a basketball game, a football game, or whatever sport it might be. There are so many opportunities to help a young man grow. To me coaching is a sacred responsibility. I have an opportunity to pour my life into a developing young person at a crucial time in their development. If all I talk about is winning and losing then shame on me. Life is bigger than that. You need to recognize how to win. You need to understand how to lose. And you need to recognize the lessons in both. You should have some fun doing that along the way.

There is no secret formula. I think most coaches understand that at some level you have to be able to laugh not just with the kids but at yourself and allow them to laugh at you. That's just part of life. You're not always going to do right. You're not always going to do the right thing. If they see that you can laugh at yourself, the more it allows them to see that it's ok to laugh. The more you can do that, the better it's going to be.

I have two sons that I coached. If you asked Dru if I coached him any differently than any other kid, he would say a resounding yes. And I did. I felt like I had to be harder on him because I didn't want anyone to thinking that he was given anything that he didn't earn. His playing wasn't just a function of him being with LeBron, or riding on LeBron's coattail, or me trying to package them. I wanted him to experience and understand that it was about hard work. I wanted everybody to see his work ethic… that he worked hard for what he had. When he made a mistake I was hard on him. And honestly, I was close to ruining our relationship. I learned that it was his dream and that he wanted to play basketball as much as LeBron and anybody else on that team. I realized that I needed to support him in the dream and not beat him down to the level that I was beating him down. No matter how hard I was on him, those outside of the team was never going to understand or believe that he earned anything on his own. It was always going to be because I was his dad and I was the coach. Once I got to that point, I was able to ease up on him and we became much closer after that. With my younger son, Dru helped me. I wasn't as hard on Cameron but I got to the same point with him. Going to his junior year, he should've been the point guard. At first I had two seniors ahead of him and I was going to start Cameron because they were ahead of him. But

Dru helped me understand, 'Hey, Dad. This is the same thing. No matter what you do, you gotta do what's best and right for the team.' I had to make a tough decision. One of the families stopped speaking to me for a while, and they had been with me since their son was in the fourth grade, all because I started Cameron ahead of their son. They recognized as the season went on that it was the right move. And I always say it's not who starts the game but who finishes and their son finished the game. It was the right decision and Cameron led us to a Final Four appearance. We didn't win it but we played against a great team that had two NBA pros on it in Daequan Cook and Norris Cole. But if we hadn't made that decision to start Cameron we wouldn't have gotten there. Those types of decisions are hard for any parent.

    The great thing about the relationship with Bron is we started when he was 10 years old. He was just a young man looking to be a part of something. When he saw the commitment we had to basketball, he recognized he was pretty good at it. But I think it was bigger than he was pretty good at it. He saw the sacrifices I made to all of them. I'd pick them all up before practice and we'd practice. We'd drive from Akron to Cleveland, just to find a place to practice. Just the fun that these guys had together was always more about just basketball.

    With that being said, I saw him when he couldn't make a lay-up. I saw him when he struggled shooting the ball. I watched that development happen. It was a special time. I was focused on the team. I didn't treat him any different. I always recognized he was better. Did I recognize he would be the best player on the planet at 10 years old? No. Did I recognize that at 14? No. Did I understand that at 17? I thought he would be a good NBA player but I thought he would struggle at first. So he surpassed every expectation that I had. I knew that he was going to get there but he got there so much faster than I envisioned him getting there. Ten years in, he's won four MVPs. That just speaks volumes to the talent, the abilities and the work ethic he's always had. He's always had that work ethic from the time he was 10 years old.

His first two years in high school, I was the assistant coach. The last two years as the head coach. He missed one practice. That doesn't happen, especially in high school. We don't take days off. We practice Saturdays and Sundays. We don't take days off, especially with that group. They wanted to be in the gym so we opened the gym up every day. All that time he put into it, you appreciate the rewards he's gotten because you know that he earned them. There's nothing that's been giving to him. He worked for everything. It was just a fun ride and was great to be a part of it.

Dru Joyce II has been the head boys basketball coach at St. Vincent-St. Mary's in Akron, Ohio, for 15 years. He is best known as LeBron James' high school coach and winning two state championships. He also coached his two sons, Dru Joyce III and Cameron Joyce at St. Vincent-St. Mary's.

BEFORE YOU CAN TEACH, YOU GOT TO REACH
GANON BAKER

The core values from some of the great coaches that I had in my life centered around tremendous passion. Passion drives intensity, determination, and hard work. This is not just basketball. I've had soccer coaches and little league coaches that instilled some amazing things in me. Coaches that have passion for what they do demand focus and concentration at an early age and a late age. Any time a coach has passion and energy, that's contagious.

They were not just about winning or losing. They want you to do your best and a little bit more. I try to teach coaches that right away. I tell them that life is too short. Our days are numbered. These kids and parents have other things to do if they are not going to get all of you. I tell them to soul search and see if they really love it because if they love it, everything else is going to be a lot easier and more fun. The kid will get better because they want to. Before you can teach them, you got to reach them. You have to connect.

The other thing is coaches taught us something. Do it or I'm going to run you is not coaching. That's discipline. That's slave driving. A great coach taught me. So when I went to the gym, my body went to the gym but my mind went to the gym too. They really explained things and demonstrated things so that I retained better. A great coach is a great teacher.

A lot of my coaches had a charisma. They understood the players. They were what we call a player's coach. They wanted to connect with the players and make it more about the relationship so they can each get out of it what they want. It might be getting behind them and pushing them, metaphorically. It might be getting in front of them and pulling them, metaphorically. It might be walking with them. It might be buying a kid a shake after a bad game. It's kind of hard to teach that to coaches. It has to be in them. But they can develop that within themselves if they do some soul searching.

I've been training kids since I was 18. I'm 41 now. I've had parents, kids and NBA players call or tell me, 'I was mad as heck at you but now I understand what you were trying to do. Thank you for sticking with me and believing in me. Thank you for not letting me be less than what I can be.' It validates me in being real. A great teacher sometimes makes you uncomfortable so that you can be outstanding. You can't be comfortable and outstanding. So sometimes you have to go through stuff and break stuff to get the good stuff. It builds and develops you as a player and as a person.

Character is something you can teach as soon as a kid walks in the gym. It's your whole training environment. It's body language. It's how you treat people. It's how you talk to the janitor. It's random acts of kindness even during practice. Character is everything that encompasses practice. You acknowledge that in front of the team. You acknowledge that to them individually.

I had a high level player in the NBA constantly spit on the floor. We were at an NBA arena, a very historic NBA arena, and after the second time he did it, I just had to stop and say, 'Dude, that's disrespectful to the game. It's disrespectful to the floor. There's a lot of reasons why that's not good. Clean it up.' He looked at me like I was nuts but I don't think anyone had ever said that to him before. So he cleaned it up and I told him that he's now respecting the game and the game will stay with you. I teach kids that what you disrespect moves away from you and you can't access. But what you respect stays there and you can access it. You never know who's watching you and you never know who you can help. Make sure that you respect everybody. You can do that in a practice environment more than you can do that at home sometimes. I think it's the coach's responsibility to teach them how to be winners at life. Character is huge. There is a need for it now more than ever in sports.

Coaches nowadays are having to become parents. They have to, especially in the African-American community where a lot of young males are growing up without a dad in their lives. I think about that every time I train a kid. I might be the only male figure that he respects. For those two or three hours I have them, it's not like it's science or social studies – no disrespect to those subjects. But they love basketball. They all want to become great and they all want to play in the NBA. Maybe there is some mentoring there I can do on and off the court. That's why coaches have to choose their words wisely. Their words can really build that kid up or they can tear that kid down. I think coaches now have to be ready for the responsibility. It's more than just coaching. If you think it's just coaching you are really disrespecting your platform and you're really not getting everything you can out of that coaching position.

Ganon Baker is founder of Ganon Baker Basketball where he trains and develops more than 3,000 players a year. Players he's worked with include Kobe Bryant, Chris Paul, Vince Carter and Amar'e Stoudemire. A Nike Basketball trainer, Baker has more than 50 bestselling instructional DVDs and conducts camps and development programs around the world.

COMPLACENCY CAN GET YOU REPLACED
SHARMAN WHITE

I've always believed in hard work for everything. That was instilled in me by my mother and my father. When it came to academics, I wasn't a rocket scientist but with hard work people couldn't tell that I wasn't. It wasn't because was natural but it was because I worked at it. I try to instill that in my teams. That's my mantra for coaching… 'Put in all the hard work and sacrifice and good things will happen.'

It's worked for me. I've seen it work for the kids I've coached. I've seen it work for fellow coaches that I mentored. I've seen it time and time again and there is no substitute for it. You have to be diligent and persistent in trying to be the best.

Unfortunately in this day and age, hard work is a skill now. It's not something that kids just have. You have to tap into it. I've seen kids that started at one level and by the time we finished with them they were high level kids. It's all because they decided to work hard to reach the goals they set for themselves. I tell kids all the time that playing hard is a skill. That used to be the one thing that you knew you were going to do when you stepped on the court coming up. But now you don't know what to expect. So you have to nurture that skill of hard work.

As a coach, a mentor, a big brother, a father figure, you have to fight that sense of entitlement sometimes. It's what can you do for me instead of what can I do to make it happen.

It's an on-going process because they get complacent. I often say complacency can get you replaced. Once you get to a level of success, there are still things that need to happen to maintain that level of success. I love the John Wooden quote that says, 'Ability will get you to the top, but character will keep you there.' I believe that.

Character is what you do when no one is watching. Reputation is what other people think of you. Character is who you are. You can be defined as a hard worker but you have to be willing to work hard all of the time, not just when people are watching.

As I mature as a coach, I see a lot of things differently. Adversity is a part of everything you do when you're chasing something. As you see more situations as a coach and you see them more prevalent, you start learning how to deal with certain situations. I'm a firm believer of God and I know that things happen for a reason. He uses every situation to grow you.

Being able to get through it is the reward. Let's say your best player goes down with a major injury. You're left to keep the guys together and keep everything going.

This year, we had a player die the day before we started our first official practice. That was unchartered waters for me as a coach. Even though I had not been through this particular situation, I think that growth from other situations helped me. Now, it's growing me to another level. So we rallied together and dedicated this season to him.

I use my experiences to help as many coaches as I can, especially younger guys. But I've mentored older guys too. I try to share all of those experiences. I speak for Nike at their clinics and I speak, locally, at a lot of banquets. I'm still growing in the process. And even when people are gearing up to hear what I have to say, I'm still trying to learn in that.

Ultimately, the goal is to leave an imprint on the people you encounter. I am passionate about that with my players. I want them to be able to say the relationship they had with me as a coach made a difference in their life. We were able to use basketball to make a difference in their life. I can look at my success and I can take it as a selfish standpoint and say that I'm successful. But I've always wanted to be great. When you want to be great, it has to involve other people. The greatness and the legacy? I want that to be put beside my name but only because of what I tried to help other people do.

Sharman White is head boys' basketball coach at Miller Grove High School in Lithonia, Georgia. He has led the school to six consecutive state championships from 2009-2014 becoming the first coach and school to accomplish that feat. He was named USA Today Coach of the Year in 2014.

THE MAKING OF A NAME
LUTE OLSON

In coaching, success is all too often determined by wins and losses. I think the key to success is the effect that you have on young people with whom you're working and the community that you're in because you determine what kind of role model you are. Are you creating a positive situation in which other people can react in a more positive manner?

I'm more concerned with the effect I have on my players five, 10 years down the road than I am immediately. Because sometimes you have to drive them hard and they may not appreciate what's happening at the time. But I think your success needs to be evaluated later in terms of what effect you really had on your players.

It's happened so many times with kids that I coached. We might not have had the kind of relationship where they could say, "I know that guy is really trying to do the best that he can to help me grow from a kid to a man." But it happens a lot where guys come back that are so positive now that at the time I was coaching them were not.

In our recruiting there are some very basic things that we follow. Number one is that good people will find a way to be successful. We're not interested in recruiting players who are not good people because we know in the end good people are going to get it done and bad people are going to ruin your program.

I speak to a lot of businesses and you take a bad person and think that he's going to represent you or your business the same way that you would, you're kidding yourself. I think the same is true in athletics. We have to have complete trust and confidence in the kids in our program. We can't be with them 24 hours a day and we tell them straight up the first time we're in their home recruiting them that to be a basketball player at the University of Arizona, you're going to have to be willing to live in a glass house. You're not going to be able to do what other students do. You're going to have to be a role model. We're going to demand that. We're going to require you to participate in the community. If we don't start with good people, they're not going to be willing to do everything that we're going to require of them to do.

Part of what's required is being engrafted into the University of Arizona basketball family. We try to do almost everything together as a program. When players get together, they usually go out to the movies, go to dinner or go over one of the player's home just to have a barbeque or just to hang out.

We try to do a lot of things at my house to develop that family atmosphere. The assistant coaches.. two of them are married and have two kids. We want them at whatever event we're having, plus our secretaries and trainers and team doctor and anybody else that's involved with the program. This is truly a family atmosphere. A family atmosphere is important to the kids, especially when they're away from home. So they do have a family away from home. That's a very big part of what we try to do.

I lost my dad when I was about to be five. He died of a stroke suddenly at 47. I didn't have a dad in the family. My mother was very family-oriented. Thank goodness we had uncles, aunts and cousins around us. My grandfather, on my mother's side, lived with us too. So we had a very nurturing family situation.

I had two brothers and a sister. My oldest brother was killed in a traffic accident when I was five so I didn't really get to know him at all that well. My brother who's four years older than I and my sister who is eight years older than I were very close. We were a very close family all around.

We were competitive too. I was involved in athletics from the time I can remember. I grew up in a small town in North Dakota, so we started with basketball and baseball, probably in about the fourth grade. When I got to the seventh or eighth grade I got into football. But I was very competitive and my brother was an athlete. We were very competitive with each other.

Whatever there was to be competitive about, we were that way.

Grand Forks, North Dakota, was a town where everybody knew everybody else. The town had only 1,800 people and was very sports oriented. It was a great community in which to grow up because you had a chance to participate in just about everything, not just athletics, but I was in the band and I sang in the choir. It was the kind of opportunity growing up that you wish every kid had. But as I've gone through recruiting and have seen the lack of opportunities the kids have, I'm very thankful and grateful for the opportunities that I had when I was young.

I think now, unfortunately, there are a lot of kids that end up in single parent homes and the school environments are not always that good from the discipline standpoint and the opportunities for these kids. I think kids really feel they need to be a part of something. Unfortunately for a lot of kids in the cities, being a part of something is being a part of a gang or something negative, rather than having the opportunity to be a part of something positive like a musical group or athletics like I had the good fortune to be a part of.

But I think down deep, these kids want the same things that kids a number of years ago wanted. They want direction. They want love. They want people to care about them and show an interest in what they're doing. I think they're craving direction and discipline. I think there's too little of that for our kids growing up.

I think we as coaches need to be aware of some of the things these kids have to go through. My master's degree is in educational psychology and I'm thankful for that because you really need to understand the environments kids come from and the behaviors they exhibit.

Every kid is different. For example, in my family, we have five kids. Every one of them is different. It's the same gene pool. They grew up in the same environment and still they're as different as night and day. But we still have to recognize the differences and we have to adjust for that. That doesn't mean you don't draw the line in the sand so they know exactly where they stand. But it takes a little bit more from us coaches now because if we're demanding on players on the court, they need to know that you're doing that because we want them to be the best that they can be and like I say, 'It's not a democracy on the court. It's a dictatorship.' But then we work very hard to make sure they know we're doing that for the right reasons. And when we're away from the court, we try to be accessible to them as we can to show them that we're half-way human anyway. That's why it's important to have that family atmosphere so that they know that they're a part of something, that they're loved and respected as individuals. But we're going to be demanding because we want them to be the best that they can be. That's what families do.

Things have certainly been more difficult since my wife, Bobbi, died of ovarian cancer.

She was very active in everything we I did. She traveled on all the road trips. She rode on the bus. She was known as the team mom. Everyone called her Mom O. She was with the team and me throughout.

But the nice thing is that four of our five kids live in Tucson, 10 of the grandchildren live within 10 minutes of me. One of my daughters, Jodi, and her husband, John, who have two children away at college, live with me. Jodi has grown up in this environment just like the other children have and she has kind of taken over.

The other girls and my son haven't known anything other than this since they were young. Even when I was on the high school level, we tried to have the same type of atmosphere where we were all together as a family.

It has been an adjustment but the family has been there.

When you're unable to spend that time together, it makes you really appreciate the times that you do have. When I see my children with their families, I see the same kind of thing that me and Bobbi had. You don't see dad going off doing his thing. You see mom and dad with the kids. That's the way it's always been with my family and the people in Tuscan know that's the way it's going to be.

Lute Olson was inducted into the Basketball Hall of Fame in 2002. He spent 25 years as the head coach of the University of Arizona men's basketball team, where he won the National Championship in 1997, 11 Pac-10 titles, was Pac-10 coach of the year seven times and led his team to five Final Four appearances. He announced in 2008 that he was retiring from coaching.

A SHOT OF CHARACTER
HOMER DREW

I remember the single most time that one of my players showed character. Jamie Sykes threw a pass three-quarters of the length of the court to Bill Jenkins. Bill caught the ball between three Ole Miss defenders and threw it to (son) Bryce (Drew). In one motion, Bryce took the three and it went in. He fell to the ground. I didn't know what happened. I didn't know if he ran into a defender, if he got knocked down or if he was trying to avoid somebody.

But after the game, as we were walking out of the gym, I asked him what happened. He said, "The floor was the closest place that I could get to say, 'God, thank you.'" That brought tears to a dad's eyes. That showed character. That showed what Bryce was really about.

That shot against Ole Miss during the 1998 NCAA Tournament put us into the Sweet 16 that year. The team finished the year in the Top 25 for the first time in school history. It was a great team with a lot of character. (The shot) was played over and over on ESPN and other highlight shows. It even won an ESPY.

Character is who you are. It's what a person is. It's not their reputation or what people think about you. Character is reflected in a person's actions. For me, my strongest character traits are honesty, humility and the inner faith I have. They make me who I am. Character is really the sum of your personality.

I know that I have a deep belief in God and that allows me to have an inner peace and want to help people develop into people with character.

One day, the team was eating breakfast at a hotel in Arizona during our first trip to the NCAA Tournament. When we were about to leave, the waitress came over to me and said she wanted to compliment me on the team.

"You guys are such gentlemen. They have good manners and are respectful." the waitress said.

That meant the world to me. In coaching, you want to help people grow - not just on the court but off the court as well. You want them to be able to handle obstacles, grow and control the ups and downs of life and become good citizens. I think you really learn that over time. It's like when you hire an assistant coach. You think the person has good character. But you really learn who that person really is in time.

I think the wonderful thing about the world of sports is that your character is tested. Some people can't handle winning very well. Some people can't handle losing very well. But it's about growing and learning who you really are. You begin to develop your character when ups and downs come. How are you going to handle them? Sometimes that takes work. You have to have passion for whatever you do. The thing I hate is a lazy person. To be a success you really have to develop your character, you have to have energy. You have to have passion.

Michael Jordan is the greatest player of my generation that I've seen play. He had that energy and passion. I've heard some of his teammates like Steve Kerr say, "The same way he played in games is the same way he practiced." That tells me something about who he really is.

Oftentimes it takes being around people like that to help you develop similar character. I got into coaching because basketball was so good to me growing up that I wanted to give back to it and I wanted to be able to help people develop character in the process.

Have I been successful? I'm still trying to be successful. I don't think you can ever stop trying to be successful.

I did get a call from one of my players. It was the first time a player did this. It was about 10:30 at night. He said he wanted me to know that he appreciated my making him do what was right. It felt good to hear him say that, to know that you did something right. That's what success is. When you've helped someone develop character… when you've really had an influence on someone.

Homer Drew is the former head coach of the men's basketball team at Valparaiso University in Indiana, where he led the Crusaders for 14 years and six NCAA tournament appearances. His son Bryce Drew succeeded his dad as head coach in 2011. His other son, Scott Drew, is the men's basketball coach at Baylor University.

MAKING THE BEST 'WE' WE CAN
SCOTT DREW

Faith was instilled from mom and dad going to church at an early age, accepting Jesus Christ as my Lord and Savior and developing a relationship with him. That's been the foundation for everything. We know there are going to be trials and tribulations. At the end of the day, if you're Christ-centered, and you're focused around Jesus and trying to do his work, that's all that we're called to do. At the end, when we come before him and hear, 'Well done, good and faithful servant,' I think that's what everyone longs to hear.

Every child at some point has a foundation that your parents lay down but it's up to you to have that relationship. Sometimes it happens sooner. Sometimes it happens later. I think children that respect their parents are probably able to have that relationship a little sooner because they want to honor their parents and be like their parents. Obviously like with us three kids, I'm in coaching because that's what my dad did and I respected him and I wanted to be like him. At the same time, the more and more I was around him, and the more I saw the peace that he had and the foundation that he had, the more I wanted to have that relationship myself.

When I left and came to Baylor and I was away from family and friends, I had to lean more on that relationship and trust in God.

I always loved coaching. I even coached my brother and sister's teams when I was in college. I always loved that part of it and always worked in camps and teaching. But my senior year I knew it was either coaching or law school. My dad's team was struggling so I wanted to help them. I didn't like reading that much and I know there is a lot of reading that goes into law school. So I married a lawyer and let her take care of the reading. I did the enjoyable thing which was dealing with people and got into coaching.

Normally in coaching, it's probably like your children at times, you don't know how effective you are until after they're out and they're raising their kids and you can see where they are. With us, we're helping teenagers grow and we might not see the impact until they get out on their own, have their families, have their jobs, ask us questions, seek advice, and thank us. Then we say, 'Wow. We really did have an impact.' When I say we, it's a team thing from our chaplain to assistant coaches to our trainer. Everybody pours in and tries to make the best 'we' we can. The great thing is we know that's all based on our relationship with Jesus Christ.

We all sin and we all make mistakes. But as long as we're seeking his will and trying to abide by his word and we're in his word, and if we are close to God, we have a much better chance of being successful across the board. It allows us to continue to have faith when other people might not have that anchor.

The great thing about being at Baylor University is it's a Baptist school. We're not only allowed to share our faith, it's something that people respect and encourage. We have Bible studies with our guys. We pray before and after practice. I would think that if you came to our practice it would be hard to separate the spiritual development from the basketball and the academics and all the other areas of development.

When my dad's past players go into coach or teaching, they reach out to me and tell me how much he meant to them. They come back to support him and talk highly of him. When my funeral happens one day, to have past players and people come back and say hey he helped have an impact on my family, which will have an impact on the next generations, would be the biggest reward we could get. And the most important thing with that would be spiritually. I'm where I am today because the coaching staff helped me grow and allowed me to grow.

Scott Drew is the head men's basketball coach at Baylor University. He also served as an assistant coach under his dad, Homer Drew, at Valparaiso University. When the elder Drew retired, Scott took over at Valpo for a year before leaving for Baylor in 2003. He led the Bears to two Elite Eight finishes and the 2013 NIT Championship. Brother Bryce is head coach at Valpo.

RESPECT WITHOUT FEAR
FRED WILLIAMS

I think the moment I stepped on the floor and was practicing with players, guarding Cheryl Miller every day, guarding Cynthia Cooper every day, and being able to mix it up with them, I saw that I was more of a motivator on the floor. When you have the energy as a coach to be out there with them and to be able to feel the same movement and patterns, I get better feedback from them and they get better feedback from me. That just helps escalates the players' abilities to get better.

Over the years, players have changed a lot. But some of the messages stay the same. For example, I always tell my players respect without fear. You can respect your opponent and their abilities but never fear them. The other message that has been consistent for 30 years is, 'Coming together is a beginning and staying together is a process. But working together is success.' I think that goes back to Henry Ford and one of his quotes.

In 1984, Cynthia Cooper and I were playing one-on-one after practice and sharing moves in the open court. I shared a few things that I thought she could use. The next game, she came down the floor against some traffic, split two players, went between her legs and behind her back and scooped it up with her left hand. It brought the whole house down. I realized she bought in to what I was saying. It makes me feel good. It's just like winning a game. It's a victory. A lot of these ladies I've coached over the years, I've been a percentage of their success. But to see them go on and prosper and say good things about you in the newspaper and all that, sometimes that's more gratifying than money.

The only things that have been different from college to the pros are there are a lot of things that you have in place in college like study tables, grades, and as coaches you become like lawyers. You have to document everything that you do to the NCAA. In the pros it's much different. You coach, you practice, you fly and you play. You get to coach. On both levels, there's a lot of pressure. Everybody wants to win and you have to win quickly, especially on the pro level.

Teamwork is very important in winning. The first thing is communicating with each player on the team from the best player to the player who doesn't get a lot of minutes for you. They have to trust that you are going to put them in a situation to win a ball game but also in a situation to improve themselves each and every day. I've always told player to keep their value up every day. No matter what you do, you have to keep your value up. You never know if you're going to be traded. You never know when you're going to get that call to be in a starting role or to get more minutes. Many players in my lifetime have bought into that.

The special moment for me was in 1984, the second national championship at Southern Cal. Nobody had really done back-to-back at that time. I think we were one of the first teams to do that. It was a very special team with special players who bought into the things that we were teaching them. Every player is different. You want players to be hungry and feisty for a lot of things and that is to be a champion. You want them be a champion as a team but also as an individual. I tell players to this day to fight battles that matter. Fighting these other battles that don't matter only gets in your way. It's important to me for them to be focused and set goals.

Fred Williams is head coach of the Tulsa Shock of the WNBA. Prior to this season, he spent six seasons with the Atlanta Dream, including leading the team to the finals in 2013 as head coach. Williams also coached with the Utah Starzz, the Charlotte Sting, and the University of Southern California women's team, which won back-to-back championships in 1983-1984. He also served as a scout for several NBA teams.

RECIPE FOR SUCCESS
STEVE SMITH

The main thing with us is really getting those guys to be successful when they leave here. We don't just want people to say they were great players at Oak Hill. We put a lot of emphasis on developing the total person while they are here. That matters more than the wins and losses.

There are a lot of examples of guys that we've seen grow up before our eyes that we've been very proud of. Jeff McGinnis is one that came to mind. He's from Charlotte, N.C. He came to us for his junior and senior year. He was really a street, city type kid who everybody said wasn't going to make it. He went on to North Carolina and played in the NBA. I don't know if that would have happened had he not been here. He's just one but there's a lot of them.

One of the things that's unique with us is that we're here with them. We don't just see them from 3-5 (p.m.) like regular schools. We're here with them living on campus. We get to see them come through, grow and mature and develop as players and people. I didn't expect to be here as long as I have but I enjoy my job and I enjoy what I do. You feel like you are helping young people. So when you find a place like that, the grass ain't always greener on the other side. People always say why don't you go to college, why don't you do this? But I really enjoy what I'm doing here. It's been a lot of self-satisfaction watching these guys go on and do well.

My dad was a coach. From about the second or third grade on I used to sit on the bench and keep stats, shag towels, and get water for the guys. I always felt like I wanted to coach. I always respected my dad and felt like he made a difference with the people he worked with and young men he worked with. He was at the small college level. That kind of got me going at a young age where it just always seemed like I wanted to coach and teach because that was what my dad did. Ever since I could remember that's what I wanted to do. I don't know what I would do if I couldn't coach. Who knows? I played sports growing up so I am a sports fan.

Success is hard work and dedication. It's desire. I think it's something you have to work at. Some people want to be successful but they don't want to work at it. It's not going to fall in your lap. We've been good here for a long time. Our program has been stable. I've been here for a long time. We just seem to attract good players but it is hard work to be successful. If you are disciplined and you put the time in, you got a chance to be successful.

I don't know if it's wins or losses, but when I saw our kids doing so well that's when I considered myself successful. I see some other schools similar to us trying to have the same programs and you look at their kids and you say wow! They've had like three kids play Division I basketball and we had over 100. Maybe they've had kids that were capable of it but maybe they didn't get the most out of them or they weren't the right type kids or they didn't do well academically. But our program is set up for our guys to succeed. It's basically basketball and academics here. We stress that and when they get on later in life they seem to do well. You have your few here and there where you say that kid didn't make what he should have out of himself, but for the most part if you give them a foundation and a background something that's good for them with a lot of discipline, they'll be successful down the line.

I try not to say negative things. Sometimes you want to get a point across to a player but I try not be negative. I try to handle each player individually. But I try to stay away from calling a kid a failure or anything remotely like that. I think you have to remain positive. You have to pick up you players and criticize in the right way.

Chemistry and getting guys to play together will also make you successful in the long run. Team is a family anyway. The closer you are, the team has a tendency to dig down deep when things get tough or the game's on the line and the players know that they will go to bat for each other and the coaches too, then you have a chance to do something good. That is very very important with teams. It's usually the individuals that get together to make the best team, no matter what sport it is, and get the right chemistry, who are usually the ones that have the most success. It's got to be the right combination of a lot of things to make it work and to make the team function as one.

I tell my guys have character don't be a character. It's important to have guys with the right thought process. It's the same with coaches.

Some people do jobs for five or six years and get burnt out. They say this ain't for me. I've always enjoyed coaching and working with people. And when you get somebody to call back and say, "Hey Coach, thanks for working with me and working with me," or "Those three years were the best years of my life," and "I don't know what I would have done had I not been in your program." Not everybody is going to do that. But when it gets on down the line and they realize that coach had my best interest at heart and the things that he was teaching me and the discipline that he wanted me to have, that's what I have now. It means a lot to me.

I leave them with this… Give it your all. It's kind of cliché but try to be the best you can be and make a difference, not just in a game or a season but for your entire lifetime. Make a difference. I think if you do that, if you give it your all, you will be successful.

Steve Smith is head boys coach at Oak Hill Academy in Mouth of Wilson,

Virginia. He has led the school to eight national high school championships and has been named USAToday National Coach of the Year four times in 1994, 1999, 2004, and 2012. In November 2013, he won his 900th game.

MY MOM WAS MY BEST COACH
VINCE TAYLOR

The bottom line with teamwork is you are teaching them for life. Sports is a great example for life. You teach people to work together because you're going to have to do that in business and anything else you want to do. There is nothing out here where you can be successful just being alone or being a loner. You learn that early in sports because you work together to attain a common goal. With that you're going to have ups and downs and you're going to have to learn each other's personalities. When you're down, your teammates pick you up. When they are down, you pick them up. That to me is the perfect lesson with life because that's what happens.

Growing up I was fortunate to be involved in sports at an early age. You don't realize that at an early age but you start to realize how important every member of the team is to make everything work perfectly, in order to win. That was the one thing that all my coaches stressed to me, that nobody is bigger than anybody else and everybody is important. I just learned it when I was younger and as I got older I learned how much more significant that was. Each person has a job to do. If one person doesn't do his job out on the floor, the team can't win. If you have a weak link, you can lose that game. You learn different personalities. There might be a person on the team that you don't get along with. But you find ways to come to common ground for the team. It's just like in the army. If you make the wrong move, that person can die. You have to have each other's back.

The biggest thing is the journey. Nobody's going to win every game. Sometimes you learn more from losses than wins. The struggle makes you stronger. As a young kid, you don't realize that. You want to win. You expect to win. You should. But that journey and learning from the losses will make you a stronger and smarter individual.

My mother said, 'Vince, after you finish playing, you will make a good coach.' I always wanted to be a player and never thought about being a coach. But she said I was a good teacher and that I could teach them from my experiences and life lessons. She is the one that always put that idea in my head. It was a natural move for me because of my passion for basketball. I always tell my kids and any kid, if you have that passion for something pursue it. I felt like I could teach guys, not only on the court but growing up to be responsible young men. Teaching life lessons is important in a world, especially for black males, that might be fair. The whole thing is who said it has to be fair. There are going to be ups and downs and you have to be able to adjust for it. All of that and sports are connected.

A key thing I learn… I was at the University of Louisville. I was getting on the kids and the thing that woke me up one time is that a lot of kids come from single family homes where the mother is like the father or the kid is the man of the house. A lot of these kids aren't used to having a male figure tell them what to do. They're used to their mom or a female telling them what to do. They will fight against you because of that until you find ways to communicate with them. That really woke me up in coaching because I realized you can't coach everyone the same. You have to understand the background, the economic background, the home structure. Everybody is different. Everybody has different buttons to push to get them motivated. You really feel great when the kid graduates or achieves his goals, whether that is the NBA, going on to Wharton Business School, and have families or want to go into coaching.

My mother was my best coach. She coached me in the game of life to give your best, work hard, and treat everybody fairly. That's probably the most gratifying to me is to see kids doing the right thing or see them coaching and helping kids do the right thing. Most kids wonder why you are hard on them, like we do with our parents. The biggest thing is the kids say, "Now I know why Coach Taylor was hard on me.' You strive for perfection. But you never get to perfection. 'He was hard on me because he knew that I had so much more to offer.' Whether good or bad, I'm going to be there for you. Kids need you more when they are down. They don't need you when they are winning because everybody is there patting them on the back. They need to know you are there when the times are tough.

I just went through that this year. One kid on the team lost his grandfather and another kid lost his father. I said, 'Man, I know it's tough. There's not a whole lot of words to say. But I lost my mom four or five months ago and I know how it feels."

My legacy is that I was there for them, that I pushed them because I knew they had a lot of potential, and that I was always there for them through thick and then.

Vince Taylor is an assistant head coach for the men's basketball team at Texas Tech University under head coach Tubby Smith. Taylor's previous coaching experience includes coaching at the University of Minnesota, Minnesota Timberwolves, and the University of Louisville under Rick Pitino. A former professional player, Taylor is credited with being a top recruiter.

PHENOMENAL WOMEN
ADELL HARRIS

When I got the job at Tusculum, it was a program that had some conference success. They were coming off back-to-back regular season champions and had some talent returning so we had a chance to win right away and we did win right away. Initially you concern yourself with how much talent you have on the roster and do we have a chance to win. I went to some of the players' home during the summer and I asked them about each other. But every time I mentioned to them about one player, Staci Hicks from Loveland, Ohio, they were all saying that she might not come back to school because her dad was really sick. They said that with the coaching change, she might stay closer to home.

I didn't go up to see her because she wasn't a starter. She was a role player. I was honestly thinking as a coach and trying to develop relationships with the all-conference players I knew that I would have to get along with to have success. It was selfish of me early on. But they kept mentioning that she was a kid that they like but they were worried she would come back. Long story short, she did come back and after our first team meeting I told them that nothing was more important than family, God, if you believe in God or whatever your religion is, academics and basketball is fourth. I told them at any point you start to get conflicted with family life and basketball and academics, we need to have a heart-to-heart. I challenged them to come to me if they were having any of those issues. She didn't come to me after that meeting but her mom called me after the meeting and told me how her father was terminally ill and Staci was dealing with it. I told her that if anything ever happened that was priority No. 1. If she needed to get home or if I needed to find a way to get her home, I was going to be her mom's support system to get in touch with her daughter. But the kid never mentioned it to me. She was a tough kid. She worked hard and I never had an issue with her. She just did her job.

After that first call with her mom things got back to normal with our team practices. We get into our first tournament on the road in Georgia. It was a 2-game classic. We stop at a Pozole's. The bus pulls up in the parking lot. I'm thinking about the team meal, the hotel, and making sure everything is good to go and everybody was taking care of. Staci's mom calls and says that her dad flat-lined today and they didn't know if they were going to get him back. So she wanted to know the closest airport to get Staci back home to Ohio. Right away my heart kind of sunk to my stomach. I thought, 'How am I going to tell this kid, whom I've only known for about three months, that this may be happening and how I could support her best." Her mom didn't want me to tell her. She just told me she would call me back if it got worse. If she didn't call back, it meant he got better. She said have a good night. I didn't sleep at all that night. I didn't know if I would have to wake this kid up in the middle of the night and tell her her dad didn't make it and find a way to get her home to be with her family.

I watched her very closely that night. She was having fun with her teammates and was being a normal kid. And I'm just scared to death that she might be getting that news. I questioned whether I had developed that type of relationship where she could be vulnerable enough to be who she needs to be going through that.

That was the very first tournament of the year. Her dad made it through the year. But at the end of our season, the last regular season game, we're on the road. Staci's mom called me and said her dad told her that he was going to die today. He wants Staci to come home. She wanted me to wake her up and tell her to call her dad, which was one of the hardest things I ever had to do. She was always a kid who anticipated this happening.

I woke her up and she called home. I listened to her have a conversation with her dad. He tells her that he was going to die and he wants her to come home so he could see her. I've been prepared to score against the 2-3 Zone. I've been prepared to help develop a kid's jump shot, ball-handling skills, leadership skills and all those things. But I've never been in a situation like that.

Our job was to try to get her there as soon as possible and we did. She got there around 8 o'clock that night and he died early the next morning.

I am grateful that I was able to help her get there before he passed away and to make sure her mom felt like she had a place or a person to go to be okay. I don't know how I would be if my daughter was by herself during a time like that. I know today that there was a bond built off of that experience. While I was trying to develop those relationships, they weren't fully developed. She learned on me and trusted me with their most trusted thing, which is their family.

Our team drove up to Ohio. We were there for the funeral. We went into the conference tournament and we won the conference tournament. We went on to the region tournament as the lowest seed and advanced to the Elite 8 that year.

What I know at my core is I do this to help develop young ladies into phenomenal women. My thought was that God put me here to make sure they are ambitious and secure, that they're confident and understand they are beautiful and smart. That's really my message as a coach. But my message to Staci was that we are a family. When you need me, I am here for you and I will adapt and adjust to give you what you need to get through any situation. I had never been through something like that before.

My responsibilities are more than I thought they were. I think that's what God was trying to teach me. I thought it was a lot about basketball and how to motivate and inspire kids. That's par for the course but now I know there is so much more.

That season was the most success I've had as a coach. Part of it, I believe strongly, was because we came together as a family around that adversity and that tragedy for her. Those kids rallied around her and she rallied. It was special and it will always be special to me.

Adell Harris is head women's basketball coach at University of North Carolina at Wilmington. She took over the program in 2012 after spending three successful years in the same position at Tusculum College in Greeneville, Tenn. Prior to that she was an assistant coach at University of North Carolina at Ashville.

WE ARE INDEED FAMILY
CABRAL HUFF

In Georgia, there are only six state champions. If you're only goal is to win a state championship, then you may fail every year. What we try to do is ask ourselves, how are we going to make this basketball player, this student-athlete, a better person and a better basketball player from the very first time they walk in the door to the last time they walk out the door? That's my number one thing. Can I make them a better man on and off the court?

The second thing is help them use basketball to pay for their education. It doesn't matter if it is D-I, D-II, NAIA, D-III and I know they don't give scholarships, or JUCO. If you have the ability to use basketball to pay for your education, take advantage of that.

The last thing is to develop mental toughness and a sense of brotherhood. Too many times in our society it's all about I and me. We try to instill a sense of family in our guys and it's worked so far. We have our alumni come back to watch our games. It doesn't matter whether they've been out of school for four, five, six years. They come and watch games and even in the summer. The mental toughness piece is what we do in practice, is done through making sure they are taking care of their school work, just being all around tough. If you can't get through what I'm putting you through in a basketball practice or what's going on in school, how are you going to survive in a world when everything is thrown at you at one time?

We use basketball to instill those things because all of us know that basketball can be taken away from you at any time. So what have you learned other than those skills on the basketball court?

When I was a junior in high school, I got undercut on a dunk attempt. I came down on my hip and thought it was a regular hip injury. I went to the doctor and come to find out I had a benign tumor on my hip my whole life. If I hadn't found out about it at that time, I would have had to have reconstructive hip surgery at the age of 22 or 25, somewhere around there. So that was a blessing in disguise. Basketball led me to that and I'm a better person because of it.

Last year, we made it to the state championship game. But through it all I was going through a divorce. Basketball was the thing that kept me sane. When you lose someone you had been friends with and spent eight years together, it's tough, no matter what the circumstances. So basketball and my players were important to me in that process.

I also bring guests in to speak to the team about adversity and life, what they had to overcome things in their life. We also take a practice day and we sit down and talk about different things, including adversity. We ask them about the toughest things they've experienced? We, as a coaching staff, also share the tough things that have happened in our lives. It helps us bond as a family and helps them understand that we have gone through adverse situations that helps us understand our players more. Whether you realize it or not, kids may be going through difficult times and shielding it because they don't think people can relate. It's a saying that people use a lot but it's true… 'Kids don't care how much you know until they know how much you care.' So for us to be able to connect with them on that level, it shows that that they can overcome anything and still be effective.

That's part of us being a family. We don't try to hold things back. My team knows that I went through a divorce and how adverse it was. Maybe there is someone who dies in a family. Or someone doesn't have enough money to do something. We as a team talk about those things and talk about them so we can help one another get through it. We refer to each other as brothers and we reach to ourselves as family. Before a game or after a game, we say, '1-2-3 Brothers! 4-5-6 Family! 7-8-9 State Champs!" We feel that with everything that we're doing we are state champs. But we also know that the first two things come before being a state champion. If we don't get to that last point, we're still brothers and family.

Cabral Huff is head boys basketball coach at St. Francis High School in Alpharetta, Ga. He led the school to five state tournament appearances, including runner-up, three Sweet 16s, and the school's first state championship in 2014.

THERE HAS TO BE BALANCE
DARRYL SHARP

    I'm kind of an old-school guy when it comes to recruiting. I like to see the foundation that the parents have set. I reach out to the parents with the initial process, maybe two or three times. And then I'll talk to the kid maybe once. I want to see what mom and dad have instilled in the kid early. A lot of coaches today recruit the kid and the AAU coach. I put the kid and the AAU coach into the equation but I want to know what's going on at home. Has mom instilled discipline? Has mom put good values into the kid? Are they spiritually connected? Is that important? Those are things that are very important for us at Hampton University.

    Character is very important. You want kids who have good values and morally strong and were raised in that type of environment. With good character typically means good work ethic, the discipline piece becomes easier and understanding what expectations are. That translates into the classroom as well. Typically if you have good students in the classroom, you're going to good students with high IQ on the court.

    My high school coach had that kind of impact on me. It was a different time. I'm 46 now so I think the expectations in the early to mid-80s were a lot different compared to our youth today. There was a stronger work ethic then. I think the key today is you have to have some discipline. You have to be committed. With discipline and commitment and seeing how important it is to be a team.

    I was recruiting a kid and he says to me, 'Coach, can you make me a pro?' I said, 'No, I can't make you a pro.' When you talk about less than half of a percent of all college basketball players will have a chance to try out for an NBA roster, that's a small group of people. Only five percent of high school athletes will play Division I. You have a better chance of running out and getting struck by lightning on a sunny day than you do of making it to the NBA. I'm not killing dreams because everybody should have a dream. But you should also understand what the odds are of that dream becoming reality. So I wouldn't go to school counting on those types of odds.

I don't give kids a sales pitch. I ask the kid if Hampton a place they want to be academically and socially. They say, 'Coach, you haven't said anything about basketball.' I let them know that's a given. But if you got hurt tomorrow and tore your ACL, would Hampton be a place you want to be, academically and socially? This is the place that you are going to be shaping the most critical time in your life, between 18 and 22. You are transitioning from being a young adult at 18 to a responsible and independent adult at 22 years old. Socially and academically, can Hampton and the coaching staff help provide that to you? If those two things are in place, the basketball piece you are really going to be happy with.

I believe in life there is a balance. You can't put 100 percent into basketball and be successful academically. My thing is I want student-athletes. I want kids that want to come here and get an education and graduate. That's important to me. At our level, in the MEAC, which is low-major Division I basketball, we're not producing a lot of pros. Are you going to be a pro in life? Are you going to be able to go and get a job and one day get married, have a family, and be a responsible black male? That's what I teach and nurture off the court.

If I do the job that I know I can do, then they will call me a year from graduation, two years from graduation, five or six years from graduation and tell me they're getting married and they want me to attend. If they respect me and they look to me as a big brother or a father figure who helped them during their pivotal years, 18-22, that'll happen. That means I've had an impact on their lives.

Darryl Sharp is has been an assistant coach at Hampton University for the past five seasons under coach Edward Joyner Jr. He handles recruiting, opponent scouting, and managing the team's academics. Sharp also worked at Iowa State, Norfolk State and Louisville.

JUST A GOD THING
JAMES NAKAMURA

    Knowing who Christ is your life, living it and walking it for him, is what success is for me. I look at basketball and coaching the same. I like to win, don't me wrong. But my definition of success is that I have imprinted something of character, strength, and something of Christ in each player. That they would grow to be the man of God that God desired them to be.

    We were in the East Coast Homeschool Championship last year. We lost our best player. We were struggling and fighting and it was a close game the whole way. At the very end of the game, I call a final timeout. God impressed something really powerful on me and I said something to the guys. I got a little choked up when I did it but I said, 'We're down by five points. We're going to execute. We're going to do what we planned. But I want you to know with a minute left, win or lose, you guys are champions to me." I had them for two years. I got to know them. They were great kids, with great character. They work hard. They fought hard. They played as a team. They treated each other as a family. That's what was going to be more powerful to me.

    It's so rare that people are going to get a stint in the NBA and live that basketball dream. But if they can learn great life lessons thru it then I feel successful as a coach and in the game of basketball.

    At the college level, we do want a certain level of character to start with. But we do want to see them progress. We are all on a journey. We're all at different places and have different areas to grow. Being able to handle adversity, understanding the value of hard work, honoring your teammates, to live as brothers in Christ… those are the areas of character development I would like to see in all of us.

The kids buy in. On the college level, I coach at a Christian college, so it's all there. We integrate it so we're not as explicit as saying, 'Here is the life lesson. It's going to help you in your walk." But I think especially for high school and college-age men they want to see it lived out. They don't want words. Words are less value than living it out. We live it. We model it. We ask for forgiveness when we fail and screw we up, which we do. We're very honest and we're real with them. That's modeling it and I think that's the way it's taught. That's far more effective than let's crack open the Bible and have a 30-minute Bible study. As valuable as that's going to be and it is an important part of it, I think it's equally important and impressing and sometimes more when we model it.

For me, I became a believer when I was in middle school. I was not a great player. I had to learn a lot about the Xs and Os. I had to bring it every practice just for the privilege to sit on the bench in high school. I just loved the game. I had so mentors, a lot of men's groups, a lot of prayer along the way. That taught me a lot of things. I think it's a life lesson.

I am so thankful to God that he can take something I love, which is the game of basketball, and use me to mentor young men, to teach and coach them, and hopefully model a Christ-like life for them and walk with them through it.

Coaching was a process of God and following his lead. He just continually surprises me in where he continues to take me. Quite frankly I was never a star player. I just assumed it could be something I enjoyed and watched. But to be able to learn it, apply it and grow is just a God thing. This is something that only God can author.

James Nakamura is an assistant coach for the men's basketball team at Johnson

University in Knoxville, Tenn. Prior to that he coached the Knoxville Ambassadors high school team.

NO FEAR, NO DOUBT
MIKE DAVIS

A long time ago, I measured success by how much money I made. But after you've been in the world for a while you realize that success is not how much money you make, but how many people's lives you have touched. It's a great feeling to have a former player, a friend or someone that you don't even know come to you and say that you really made an impact on their lives. To me that's success—serving other people and helping them achieve what they want.

This summer, I spoke at a camp. When the camp was over, a coach approached me. He was comparing his story to mine about how he had a speech impediment and he feared speaking in public. But to see me on this platform and giving my testimony really inspired him to the point of shedding tears. When you're talking to a man, I mean talking man-to-man and you're sharing something that you've experienced, and begin to cry, it's such an overwhelming feeling. It's almost unbelievable that you can affect someone to feel like that.

As a youngster, I was always afraid to speak because of my speech impediment. Even as an adult, this has been a challenge. People think I'm quiet. I'm really not. It's just that I have this speech impediment and when I'm around a crowd of people that I'm not familiar with I won't say anything.

This coach at the camp could relate to that. I was just thanking God to be in this situation and to be the head coach (now at Texas Southern University). He just saw all the things that were good for me. But I also let people know that it wasn't easy.

I came from a humble background, a small town, Fayette,

Alabama, where everybody knew everyone. So if you did anything, everybody knew. There were very few secrets in this town. What I tried to do was never embarrass my family and my community. There may have been times when I did some things that no one found out about, but you try never to embarrass them.

When I grew up, my father wasn't around. He died when I was in the sixth grade. I hear so many guys criticize their fathers for not being around. I wanted my father around too. I didn't get a chance to share any of my dreams with him and he didn't to share any of his dreams with me. I think about that a lot with my children.

In my profession, it's so time consuming that whenever I get a chance I want to be with them. When I became the head coach (at Indiana University), I said, 'Okay, if I want to have them with me, I can. If I want to bring them to practice, I can.'

As an assistant coach you have to get permission from the head coach and you don't want to cross those lines sometimes because you have a job to do. Coach Bobby Knight was always good about letting my older boy come to practice and watch practice, but when I became head coach there was no limits to it.

I try to treat my players like my own boys. I get upset with them sometimes but I still love them. I push them to make them better. I'm easy to talk to. I keep the lines of communications open. I have to catch myself sometimes because you think like a coach and want to be a little critical of them, but you have to remember that they're young men. I'm growing everyday as a coach just as they are growing as players. The bottom line is I believe in them and I expect nothing but their best.

When I took over the Indiana program, I expected to succeed, I'm no different than anyone else in the profession. You always dream and think that you can coach at the highest level. But whether you do or not, success is always in the back of your mind. You simply have to find out how to get there. I was just blessed to be in a situation to achieve that. I think it surprised a lot of people because when people don't know you by name, it always surprises them. But everybody think they know the best of the best but that's not true. I'm not sure how many NBA players there are but there's a whole lot of good basketball players that are not playing in the NBA. The same thing applies to coaching, a lot of coaches get that label as great coaches but there are a lot of great coaches that coach this game that you will never hear of.

I read this book, What Makes the Great Great by Dennis Kimbrough and in it it talks about two things that prevent people from being successful… fear and doubt. When I shared my story about how God has been in my life, how he has gotten me to this point, it gives other people hope.

We all can get down on our knees and pray. They've seen what he has done for me and they see hope. How many people watched me play for a national championship and think to themselves, "One day, as a coach, I can get to that level?" If you saw Coach Krzyzewski or Coach Roy Williams coach for a national championship, it never enters your mind that you can get to that point. But seeing me, it took it to another level from just a dream to a hope.

My message is consistent. Trust God and leave everything in his hands. There is no need to be afraid or doubt. If you are faithful to him, he'll make a way for you. Some people think they have to hit the lottery for them to know that God has blessed them. But having good health and having the ability to carry on a conversation or waking up is a blessing from him.

I pinch myself sometimes because of where I am. Years ago, nobody knew my name. But I put my life in his hands and God found that he could trust me.

I came to that revelation about (17) years ago. I prayed for wisdom and knowledge for the first time, sincerely. I prayed with an open mind and didn't want anything superficial. Sometimes we pray for what we want, riches and this job and that job. But for the first time I got down on my knees and felt good about where I was. I always heard my mother say, "You want peace of mind."

I never had peace of mind because I always wanted material things, positions and money. But when I prayed for wisdom and knowledge, they were the most powerful things I could have.

I've grown so much as a coach and as a person. If you hear my first interview and hear how far I've come, that's because of that wisdom and knowledge.

Mike Davis is head coach of the men's basketball team at Texas Southern University. He had previously served in the same position at the University of Alabama Birmingham and Indiana University, where he succeeded legendary coach Bobby Knight. He led the Hoosiers to the national championship game in 2002, his second season at the helm.

COACH JESUS, TEAM DISCIPLES
ALLEN RAY

I coached a church team in Jamaica, New York, called Calvary Baptist Crusaders. The team was more like a family because with us, there was more than just basketball. It was about how basketball relates to everyday life and how that relates to your faith.

We did a lot of outreach in the community and also had kids that weren't involved in the church that participate in the basketball program. We were not trying to shove religion down their throats but we brought them to a point where they could make a decision about what they want as far as their faith was concerned.

Sometimes you got that kid that all he wanted to do was play basketball. But then there were some that started off that way and through the word of the day and illustrations we used, they began to see that what they were being taught went far beyond the court.

We had several incidents where if our basketball program wasn't involved, a couple kids might not be alive today. One parent called me and thanked me for becoming involved with her son. He wasn't a bad kid but she was a single parent and she tried to let him have his way. Others tried the same thing and their sons have failed. They experimented with drugs, got involved in gangs or father children out of wedlock.

But this lady brought her son to me because he was interested in basketball and she was trying to get him to go to a church as a way of preventing him from going the way of so many other inner city boys without fathers or other strong male role models to guide them.

I made a deal with him at the beginning that he could play basketball as long as he did two things: attend youth services at least twice a month and stay in school and out of trouble. At first he didn't want to do it. He walked out a couple times. But one time he walked out, he was surprised that one evening I showed up at his house. I had made a commitment to him. He was surprised that I did that.

We sat down, the boy, his mother and I, and had a long talk about commitment. I think he was impressed by that. I think he realized that there was someone outside of his mother that actually cared for him and it wasn't just about basketball. He got his grades together, graduated high school and now he's in the military. He's married and now has kids.

It makes me feel good to know that I have some kind of influence on somebody's life in a positive way. It also helps when I come upon other situations like that. I can tell kids that I have had other kids that have been in the same situation and that they made it. You can too.

A lot of times, they think that they are the only ones in that situation. But they're not. There are people out there who are willing to help get them out of negative situations if they want help.

Probably the main reason I got into coaching is because my friends convinced me to try out for basketball when I was 15 or 16. I wasn't very good, but I was tall and willing to do little things that others didn't want to, like rebound and play defense. But the main problem I had was I had never learned footwork to make a layup.

I tried out for the team and didn't make layups. I went to the coach and asked him if he could show me the proper footwork to make layups and he cut me. He flat out said, "No! Go home!"

At that moment, I was embarrassed but I was also determined that if I ever was in a position like that where somebody needed my help, I wasn't going to turn them away.

My personal scripture that I try to live by is John 6:37: *"All that the Father gives to me will come to me. And whoever comes to me I will never drive away."*

Our theme for the basketball ministry is I Tim. 4:12 that basically says, don't let people look down on you because you're young. You can set an example for others. I think basketball is like the perfect ministry, especially to teach about teamwork. Jesus took 12 men, trained them, taught them, then had them go out and produce.

Basketball is the same thing. You take 12 players and you train them in the system that you want them to use. You give them discipline. You give them guidance and love and then you put them out there and they supposed to produce.

I share that with the team to teach them about teamwork. But I also use Duke Coach Mike Krzyzewski's fist model that it takes all of the fingers and the thumb to make up a fist. I start off with the fist model because it's easier for them to understand. But once they get further along in the season we have a one-minute Bible study before games and they get the similarities between the basketball team and Christ's ministry on earth.

I think I've already seen the impact that I've had on players. I have guys that I coached 20 years ago, who are now in their 30s saying they're going to bring their kids to me to coach and train. That lets me know that I'm doing something right.

Allen Ray has coached basketball for nearly 30 years. He had coached 13-18 year olds at Calvary Baptist Church in Jamaica, NY.

HOME SWEET HOME
TOM BOSLEY

We're all creatures of habit. The more times you do things the right way, the better you will become at it. We talk about paying attention to detail at Southern High School. We're a program that pays attention to detail. That goes in line with our whole commitment to work ethic.

Work ethic is commitment where you maximize each and every moment that you walk in the gym with a goal in mind. The only way you can reach that goal is with a daily plan to work as hard as anybody else.

We tell our kids that there might be somebody down the road working harder than you. In order for us to win a state championship we have to work hard. We're not talented enough. We have to be the hardest working team in the state to give ourselves a chance. That's what we base our entire philosophy on.

Oakland, Maryland is a rural community. It's a coal mining town. It's a blue collar area. It's like the Pittsburgh steel mills in the old days. You crawl in a small space, sometimes three feet, four feet, sometimes all day long. That's work. We try to get our kids to understand that if those people are making sacrifices to give them a good life, the kind of life that we have in our area, then surely with the God-given talents they have they can maximize their effort and their work ethic on the basketball court on a regular basis.

We also have the same emphasis in the classroom so we don't separate these two. That's why our gym is always packed. We always play in front of a packed house. It's more than just a basketball game at Southern High School. It's an event.

The town rallies around the team. Anytime we travel we have a bigger crowd than our opponents, no matter how far we go. We went to the state tournament and had a couple thousand people from Oakland and the town only has about 1,000.

Our people understand (mining). A lot of our kids are affected by that with their parents or grandparents doing that work today. It's kind of what our community is all about. They respond very well to work. I don't know if I stopped a practice for lack of effort in years. It's kind of a ripple effect of our community. It's a real working community.

We're not some basketball factory. We very seldom have college players, for example. We spend a lot of time shaping people for the future. We know that we're not going to make money playing hoops. And we tell them that we're building them to go to college. That's a big goal of ours. We tell our kids all the time to get out of this town and go to college. It's not that we think it's a bad town, but they need to get out and see what the world is like. We're very lucky. We're in a very low crime area and a very good situation. Things are very nice here.

That makes it easy teaching life lessons because they've seen the examples and they continue to see the examples.

Every kid has a notebook. We write in our notebooks on a daily basis before we start practice or warm-ups. At a certain time every day, the whistle blows, they run to the sideline, grab their pens and notebooks and sit in the middle of the floor. We may talk about character traits, commitment, academics, or we might recognize a kid that did well. We've had the valedictorian of our school, in a graduating class of about 200 three or four times.

They write things like a message of the day that might be about having character instead of being a character, don't be average because it's the same distance from the top as it is from the bottom.

So strive for the top. Those kinds of we'll talk about on a regular basis.

They really respond. They take care of their notebooks. They write everything they can. They take a lot of pride in our program, in everything we do. We never have a problem with trying to get a kid to jump on board.

We have never told them they have to have their notebooks on the road. Yet I look back on the bus and they're looking at them. Kids are sharing ideas. They're talking about things. They're talking about effort, maximizing effort tonight. When you hear those kinds of comments coming from the back of the bus, that's a sign that some value has been placed on what you have been teaching.

When the season ends, do I see them show up a lot? No. But have I seen them show up before? Yes. I've seen a guy show a younger kid a notebook when we have our guys coach third and fourth grade kids. They go to our gyms around the community and coach them. You hear them say some things about their notebook and their continued work ethic. They try to share things they feel will have a lasting impression on younger kids.

That's how I learned my work ethic.

I grew up working. I grew up in a big family, four boys and a girl and we all worked, the entire family, the entire time.

We hitchhiked everywhere we went because we didn't have a car and the family didn't have a lot when we started. My parents worked the hardest. My dad is now deceased, but he was a workaholic. We learned how to work the right way.

If I came home after a game and complained to my dad that I didn't play much, he'd say, "I guess you have to go back and work on your game. I don't want to hear any more about it." That's something to hear as a 15-16 year-old kid. But I took that with me through college and in life.

Tom Bosley coached the boys basketball team at Southern High School in Oakland, Maryland for more than 20 years and four years at the college level.

IT'S ALL COMING TOGETHER
DARYL HOUSE

Through life, you have your tests and trials while you are young. You want to do what your mother, or your grandmother, or your father, or your coach or teacher, say. When you're young we always want to please others and be on the right track but the older we become we see that it's really about the vision that's on your heart. The God that you believe in has placed something special that only you can achieve and accomplish during your time on this earth. So it's important for you to connect with your own vision and your own dreams. From there you can step out on faith, take action, and move forward with the knowledge and wisdom that you've gained. No matter what anybody else says, you are doing it. You don't need pats on the back. You don't need trophies. You don't need a star on your homework or anything like that as long as you know that what you did today was from your heart and you put your best foot forward.

Success is having goals and making positive progress towards those goals each and every day that we have an opportunity to wake up and put two feet on the floor. Having goals is just a mile marker of where you want to be destination wise and where you are today. Your destination is whatever you have a vision of doing or whatever you have a vision of becoming or whatever you have a vision of giving, contributing for your community, family, etc. Waking up and making progress towards the goals each and every day is my definition of success. As I coach my teams, I let them know that your success doesn't always show up on the screen for everyone else to see. But as long as you know that you've made progress today and you've taken another couple steps forward towards the things that you want out of life and towards the goals that you want to complete, then you know that you are making progress.

When I was graduating from high school, I was in a position to go to college and play basketball. I was fortunate enough to play with Division I level athletes on my own team. Three out of five of our starters were Division I recruits. In the Minneapolis City Conference, we were playing against many Division I athletes on their teams as well. That was always the dream coming up at that time… to go to college, play Division I basketball or play your sport. It was some personal issues with my family at home during my junior year. I started being on my own, so to speak. I was too grown for my own good. I was too hard-headed. My parents had divorced when I was younger. So becoming an older teenager and living between my mother and my father's home, I made a lot of decisions on my own. During my senior year, I ended up getting my girlfriend pregnant. From there, my life took a turn away from my dreams and onto the track of responsibility being a teenage father. While all of my teammates and those I competed against were on their way to college, I was at home going to work at two jobs fulltime and a part-time job leaving the house when it was dark in the morning and returning when it was dark at night. I realized the decisions that I made put me on the path that I was on and it wasn't toward my ultimate dreams. About that time, when I was about 19 years old, that I started to realize that I can't follow along with what everybody else is doing, I had to focus on my dreams. It hurt. That year after high school I was working hard like a grown adult man while others were pursing their dreams. At that time, I started getting connected to myself because I had to. I was on my own.

I got into coaching about 22 years ago. I coached a sixth grade boys team that summer and we ended up going undefeated and winning our city championship in our youth league. That really turned me on to my love and passion for teaching and empowering other young people. My current high school team played in a holiday tournament and my starting point guard from that team over 20 years ago coached one of the teams that we played against. All the years of teaching and coaching are coming together. I'm humbled.

Daryl House coaches at Minnetonka Skippers High School in Minnesota. He has been serving as a head coach & mentor for youth in the Minneapolis-Metro Area for over 22 years.

SELFLESS, EDUCATED MEN OF CHARACTER AND ACTION
BOB GHILONI

We constantly talk to our players about trying to develop their character, trying to develop their basketball skills, and trying to develop their academic skills. Our whole purpose, and we have this in their notebooks, is to become selfless, educated men of character and action. In everything we do we talk about that. What we do on the floor, we want you to be unselfish. Off the floor, we do service. We work with West Licking Warriors, which is a Special Olympics team. We raise about $4,000 a year for them. We have a couple practices with them. We've gone to see one of their games this year. We'll work the Special Olympics track meet in the spring. Selfless. We read to inner city kids in Newark once or twice a year. We work with a lunch buddy program at Ben Franklin School in Newark every other Thursday where the kids are just matched up with a young man. The school has about 60 percent poverty rate and most of the kids don't have a positive role model. So our guys just go in and have lunch and have recess with them. That's it. It's not tutoring. It's not mentoring. These are third and fifth graders. It's just having a male role model hang around with you for an hour every other week.

So our guys will do about 20 hours of service every year. Some of them have picked up on it. Some have worked for Habitat for Humanity. Some through their fraternity do other service projects. It's a cool thing but I also think it's an important thing that we do together once in a while.

As far as the educated part, obviously this is a great school. But I want to make sure these guys take advantage of opportunities. I make them go to speakers on campus. Some of these guys have no idea who Madeleine Albright is. They have no idea some of the people that go through this place. I'm not into imposing into every bit of their lives and trying to run and control them. But at the same time I am into making sure they take advantage of some opportunities. And as the basketball coach they'll do it because I said so, so be it. We'll do some of that.

We had two sessions with career services talking about networking and resume writing. Next year, we're going to do an etiquette lunch with career services. Learn what fork to use, what hand to shake. It might seem like stupid stuff to some but sometimes these are things you are not trained in. But I want us to be educated in every way.

During study table, one of those three nights a week, we take a half-hour and we talk about our core values, where I bring in a speaker to reinforce some core concepts. Or I might have a senior speak about some things we need to do to be selfless, educated men of character and action. So we keep up with them academically. For the third semester in a row, we had a 3.2 G.P.A. as a team. So we were actually recognized by the National Association of Basketball Coaches as 1 of only 100 men's basketball programs in the country out of almost 1,000 that had a 3.1 or above G.P.A. for the year last year. The cool thing about it is guys are buying into it.

Not only do we have what we call our purpose of being selfless, educated men of character and action, we have something that we call the Denison Way. Our goal as being part of the Denison Way is that we pursue excellence in everything that we do. Am I crazy enough to believe that they are doing the best in everything? No. But we stress that with them. It's kind of hard for a 20-year-old to look you in the eyes and tell you he's not doing his best and you call him on it and he argues with you. They know they should be. Part of the Denison Way is also that we have a foundation of love and that revolves around us loving the game of basketball and loving each other. We might not like each other all the time. They laugh when I say that but you love each other because it means that you have respect for what each guys does every day.

Finally, we talk about having success. All we mean by success is an old John Wooden quote that says, knowing at the end of the day I did my best to do the best I could to be the best I can become. Basically, I worked against my potential every day. If that's good enough to get an 'A' that's great. If not, I can look myself in the mirror and be happy with myself.

Bob Ghiloni is head men's basketball coach at Denison University in Granville, Ohio, where he's spent 12 of his 27 years as a head coach. His first 15 years were spent at Bishop Ready High School in Columbus, Ohio.

COACHING IS LIKE MANAGING
LONNIE BARTLEY

    I played basketball all my life. I went out for the basketball team here at Fort Valley State and made the team. We weren't winning. As a matter of fact, when we went home for Christmas break we were 0-6. I knew I was going to quit because I had never been on a team that wasn't successful. During the Christmas holiday, I was thinking that I had been doing something with basketball since I was 8. So I decided that since the women's team was winning I was going to go to the women's basketball team and ask her if I could help them. I was going to do it with the men but I didn't want to be a manager of a team that wasn't winning. So I went to the women's coach first. But if she had turned me down I probably would've gone back to the men's coach and told him I no longer wanted to play but I still wanted to do whatever I could do, the book or stats or something. But she said she needed a bookkeeper and I worked my way to a student assistant and a grad assistant until I was a head coach.

    I can't imagine a day without basketball. When I first got my first basketball goal at 8, I've either played, coach, or thought about basketball every day of my life. I never quit anything. It took a lot for me to quit. But I just couldn't deal with losing those first games and we were able to laugh and talk and joke. That wasn't the way it was in high school. You could hear a mouse walk on cotton if we lost in high school. So I knew I couldn't be a part of that.

    I'm working on my book. The name of it is going to be *Management is Strictly Business*. When I went to college I didn't want to major in health and physical education or anything that was going to take me into the school system because I didn't and still don't believe that coaches and teaches are paid enough for what they do. So I majored in business administration because that industry was booming when I came to school. I loved cars. I have about 17 cars, including antiques so I thought that I probably wanted to be a business manager for Ford, GMC or Chevy, or something like that when I first came to college. I still did through college until when the coach before me was about to resign, she said I would be good at coaching. I said, 'No. I don't think coaches get paid enough money.'"

She never won a championship so I started working real hard, recruiting and working with the players, trying to get her a championship before we left because I was going out with her. When she said she was going to recommend me for the job. I thought, 'Well, it is a job!' So I decided I would take the job so I could get her a championship, present it to her and go about my business. So I thought I'd put in four or five years into coaching then I would go into business. By the time I had won a championship, she had been killed in a car accident. I just felt compelled to stay with the program because I knew what it meant to her. I stayed 29 years and just tried to uphold all the things she taught the players.

My business background made me believe I had what it took to get the most out of players. Coaching is just like managing. You have to find out what makes a person tick. If you find out what makes a person tick, they'll knock down a wall for you. But if you don't know what makes a person tick, they'll pretend they are trying to knock the wall down but they aren't knocking nothing down. They just want you to believe that they are trying. I just found out what makes players tick. My players for 29 years have wanted it as much as I wanted it. So it was easy for me to keep it going.

I hope my players say that I had a lot of passion for the game. I coached it like I played it… very hard. It's imperative for them to say that I was fair. I was fair to all my players. I never lied to them.

I've kept it 100.

Lonnie Bartley spent 29 years as head women's basketball coach at Fort Valley State University, where he became the winningest women's coach in black college history. He retired after the 2012-2013 season with more than 620 wins and 21 Southern Intercollegiate Athletic Conference Championships.

YOU HAVE WHAT IT TAKES
YOLANDA MOORE

  I started playing when I was in third grade. One of my classmate's dad was the junior high coach. He started a recreational league for elementary kids. He used to teach them the fundamentals of the game. We would play every Saturday. I didn't know anything about it. And actually he told me I was the worst player he had ever seen in his whole 15 years of coaching. I played all the way up to sixth grade when I started to get better.

  I'm from a little small town and it was just a way to really just get out of the house on Saturdays. But I fell in love with the game instantly and I had no idea what I was doing. It was an instant love affair though.

  Even at that young age, I felt free whenever I was on the basketball court. Whatever I was going through at home or whatever I was going through just dissipated when I hit the court. Nothing else mattered except just being out there and being free. As I continued to play and develop and got better at it, then it helped me to develop my confidence off the court, as a young lady. I hit a growth spurt in sixth grade and all of a sudden I was taller than everyone. So I went through that bullying phase and teased. Basketball was my refuge.

  I talk about it a little in my book, *You Will Win If You Don't Quit*. The book is my story from beginning to end in terms of playing. I also dealt with the depression, which I dealt with off and on in college. It was more prevalent after I finished playing in the WNBA and I retired. I had absolutely no idea what to do next with my life. So I went back to school, finished my degree, but I was not prepared for life after sports.

    I didn't have mentors growing up. I didn't have mentors in college other than coaches whose main concern was my performance on the court. Outside of that there was very little involvement. Once I was done with basketball and basketball was done with me, I had no identity because my identity was created through the sport. It's where I gained my confidence. It's where I learned to be strong and to be independent and to work hard. I learned that you get out of it what you put into it. So when that was no longer there, I really didn't know who I was. There was no other athlete, or so I thought, that I could reach out to who had experienced that. There was no help from the WNBA. I wasn't one of the upper echelon players so there was no one to help me transition to the next stage of my life.

    There was a lot of prayer and self-evaluation. I reached out to young ladies like me to be to them what nobody was to me. That helped me out of that situation. I found a comfort and happiness and a sense of fulfillment and purpose. Everything in our lives happen the way they are supposed to, based on our choices, and nothing happens by accident.

    In my role now as a coach, I see that I had to go that route to be the type of coach and mentor that the young ladies who are assigned to me need. I can empathize and know what they feel on a day-to-day basis.

    I was doing basketball camps and I was asked to speak a lot. I can't prepare a speech. I have to get to the venue, feel the energy of the audience, pray, and let God lead me to what they need. It always seemed that the theme was sharing my struggles. I felt like it was important that I was transparent. I felt like I had to let them know they are not alone, they are not the only ones who make mistakes, or bad choices. So I shared things that happened to me and how I felt, this is how I dealt with it and this is what I had to do to overcome it. People appreciate when you are honest with who you are.

I always wanted to coach. I tried for 10 years. I applied for job after job after job. I called players I played with in the WNBA who were coaching and former coaches. I sent resumes and nobody would bite. All I heard was what I didn't have. Well, you don't have coaching experience. You don't have recruiting experience. It was a Catch 22. How do you get the experience, if you can't get the job to get the experience? It was frustrating and I questioned God lots of times, 'Is this for me? And if it's not, can you take the desire for coaching away because it's too painful to pursue it. I'm giving everything that I have.'

It was refreshing when I applied this job at LSU-Eunice. I looked at all of the qualifications they were looking for, I accessed my own skills, and background and education. I figured all they could do is say yes or no. So I submitted my information and about a half-hour later, I finally got a call back. There was someone who wasn't focused about what I didn't bring to the table. They looked at what value I could bring to the table.

It came full circle. One of my starters has an eight-month-old son. He was sick a couple months ago. She was worried, wondering if she could go meet them at the hospital to check on her son because she knew she's be late to practice. But I told her. 'Look, I was a teenage mom. I know how hard that is. I know what that is to be an athlete and a mom and a college student all at the same time.' It felt good to be in a place where I could put myself in her shoes and she knows that I know how she feels and what she's going through because I've been there. I was her.

It's who I am. They see it every day as a single mom with four kids and a grandson. It's just me here. I don't have family here, trying to teach, and coach, and working on my Ph.D. So I have classes and administrative duties and I have all of these things I have to do and I have to be on top of my game for each one of them. I can't take any time off. They see that persistence. They see that work ethic. They see that drive.

I'm always reinforcing to them that they have what it takes. They are good enough, that they are made for this. Whatever they are going through, they can handle it.

You have to know what you want and not be afraid to express it. You can't quit when you know that this is the path that you're supposed to be on, that this is what you were designed and created to do, that you can't let the, 'No's,' stop you. I tell them that all the time. When I first got the job I asked them, 'At the end of the season, what do you want to have accomplished?' They all said they wanted to win the championship. Then if that's the goal, then this is what it's going to take. It's going to be hard and nobody's going to believe that you can do it because you only won eight games last year. You only won nine games the year before that. Nobody is going to believe you when you tell them that. Are you ready for that? Are you ready to hear the rejection? Are you ready to hear the people laugh at you? Can you handle that because that's what you're going to encounter? But when you step into that gym, you have to put in the work and give it everything you have because that's what it's going to take to achieve that goal. But even if we don't achieve it at the end of the day, you can still feel good about what you've done because you've done everything in your power to make that happen.

Yolanda Moore is a two-time WNBA champion (Houston Comets) and current head women's coach at Louisiana State University Eunice. In her first season with the school, she led the team to a 26-4 record and the Miss-Lou Conference Championship. She is also author of "You Will Win If You Don't Quit".

THE SWOT TEAM
GEORGE ELLIS

There is definitely a different dynamic when it comes to AAU basketball than high school basketball. There are some pros and some cons.

Basketball was created as a tool for people to have fun, another form of recreation. So the majority of the people playing AAU basketball is playing for the pure enjoyment of the game. They're playing to be able to see other teams, go to different places to play. I know a lot of kids, especially in the inner city, have never been outside of their community. So I've seen some kids play just to be able to go to Wisconsin, Illinois, and Florida, to compete against other players from around the country.

It's more challenging to instill teamwork with AAU teams than high school teams. You have players coming from different backgrounds, different neighborhoods, different areas. A lot of players do have different agendas. They want to get noticed and get that exposure and the opportunity to get recruited by a college coach. In my experience, if you have a solid coach and you have players that just want to get better, even if their goal is to still get recruited or noticed, then you have a group that is more interested in buying into team or playing defense because they can see the bigger picture.

When you're playing 20 to 25 and even 40 games over the spring, which in my opinion is too much, I try to get them to understand the concept of one body, one team. When we talk about the faith-based side, it talks about the body being different pieces and many parts but those parts can't work unless they come together and help each other. Even in a classroom piece that we have, we refer to that particular verse in the Bible. Every player is a pivotal piece in order to build a team and getting toward that collective goal.

I try to be realistic and tell kids the truth. I think that a lot of players aren't used to facing themselves and being real with themselves when it comes to their abilities. I kind of use a SWOT analysis if you're in the business world. I'm helping kids understand their strengths. I'm helping kids understand their weaknesses. I'm helping kids understand the opportunities that are in front of them. I'm helping kids understand the threats that are out there, whether it's a transfer player or another kid with similar abilities, or factors outside of the game that can be distractions such as cell phones, social media, and the wrong influences, things that can take us out.

In my first year of coaching I had 17 kids on an eighth grade middle school team. They said I couldn't cut anybody. I had this kid that played who was very talented but he didn't want to listen to anybody. I walked into the first day of tryouts at my new high school job, and there he was. I hadn't seen this kid in five years. He's a senior now and I found out that he was in an accident and had gotten shot. It was a freak accident thing where a bullet came flying through a house and hit him in the leg. It helped him understand that the opportunity to play basketball again was a miracle that could have been taken away. So we stressed that to him so he could take advantage of that tremendous opportunity he had and hopefully continue to work on his game and himself to possibly have an opportunity to play in college.

That's what I try to do with every player, whether it's at the high school or the AAU program. I try to help them see those points of the SWOT analysis. So we want them to be real with themselves so they will know what they need to get better. And if it's something they are really passionate about, they'll make it happen. If they are receptive, we can help them.

In the end, I want them to say that they got better, not just as a basketball player, but also as a student, and as a person. I love to hear stories of kids that say they made progress.

George Ellis is a professional basketball skills coach and owner of George Ellis Basketball Training & Development LLC. He is also an assistant coach at Minneapolis North High School in Minneapolis, Minn. His Real Athletics AAU program is leadership and develop-based.

BUILT FOR BLUE COLLAR WORK
BEN HOWLAND

Work ethic is really the key. When you think about me and you think about my teams, the first thing that should come to mind is work ethic, blue collar, hard-nosed toughness.

Work ethic is something that goes hand-in-hand with success. The harder you work, the more likely that you will have success. The guys that work the hardest also somehow seem to be the luckiest.

When I try to talk to our players, I go right back to the very best players I ever coached, like John Stockton and Brian Shaw. They were both the hardest workers on the team. They had a great work ethic. Brandin Knight was that guy for us (in Pittsburgh). You look for that in recruiting and then you try to emphasize that and push that with your players, equating that to improving and being successful.

It's no different for me.

This job is every day, 365 days a year. You never leave the job. Even on vacation, I'm always thinking about it. I usually take my family to see our families for a couple weeks a year. During the year two weeks off is about it. But even then I'm still working.

I want people to see our team as one that is unselfish, very team-oriented, tough mentally and physically. There's no question that work ethic and toughness go hand-in-hand.

It's not hard to teach a team when you have a good work ethic. Take Brandin. His recognition came from being a consummate team player. You're going to get recognition when you're on a good team. That's what's being taught. We are about winning. I think that's the way it is for all our teams. I think they all understand that.

Teamwork comes down to being unselfish. Shot selection is the

No. 1 thing in our offense. Taking good shots within your team is crucial. We are at a point now where our players are coaching one another. They know what a good shot is and what a bad shot is. They get on a guy who takes a bad shot because when you take a bad shot it affects the other four guys and what kind of success they're going to have. In practice we do a lot of competition drills. Everything counts so they learn that.

We look for that in our recruits. We don't want guys that it's all about them. We obviously want them to be great but we want them to fit into the team. We want them to work at it.

Every kid wants to be an NBA player and honestly very few end up being able to be an NBA player and there are some opportunities for players oversees but getting you education is the most important thing. Someday you're going to be 35 and you're going to have 40 or 50 years of life before you and basketball is going to be done for you. Do something with your education that you enjoy doing. That's one of my big things. Find something that you're going to enjoy and be happy with it. Life's too short to go to work every day and not love what you do.

I knew that I was going to coach when I was in the sixth or seventh grade. I love basketball. I knew I didn't want to have to really *work* for a living. I wanted to do something that I liked doing. That was my focus all the way back when I was 12 years old.

I have always been involved with basketball, either as a player or as a coach. I was lucky enough to get in early because of relationships with friends. I was a graduate assistant at Gonzaga at 23, so I was involved in Division I basketball since then.

But I think the most important coaches are at lower levels, coaches that deal with kids at the elementary, junior high, and high school levels. Those are the key people who are critical in my opinion because they're teaching the fundamentals and they're getting kids to get excited about basketball and to love basketball at an early age. They should learn work ethic and hard work and that it pays off down the road. We're getting kids at the college level and we have to keep working with them for them to improve. But they should be pretty good players to begin with. They're really developing players at the lower levels.

When they're 9, 10, 11, 12, 13 years old, those are key times. If they learn work ethic then, it's like riding a bike.

When we go recruiting, we're looking for athletes, we're looking for guys that are skilled and who have a good attitude. These are guys that fit in with other teammates. There are a lot of them out there, but they're hard to get because everybody wants them.

But if you happen to get one with a good work ethic, things will work out in the end.

Ben Howland served as head men's basketball coach at Northern Arizona, Pittsburgh, and most recently at UCLA. He was named National Coach of the Year in 2002 after leading Pittsburgh to the year in school's history. He is among only a handful of Division I coaches who have led three different schools to the NCAA tournament.

MOTIVATED TO DO THIS
DON PITTMAN

I didn't start coaching to win games. I started coaching to motivate the elementary school kids that I was teaching. We had some kids that needed some guidance. They actually reminded me of me. So I started without pay. There was no money involved but it was to spend time with kids and teach them proper values, how to take care of themselves, and what manhood was really about.

Many didn't have a positive male role model in their lives. I just happened to be pretty good at it. As the years went on, I kept my same philosophy that we were playing and competing but there were some other things you needed to do to be successful besides playing basketball and winning games. It was about being a good student, being a good person, character development, and taking care of responsibilities at home. I would tell them, 'Don't go having momma call me because if momma calls me, I'm gonna go with what momma says.'

Basketball allowed me to reach into their lives and do a lot of things with them that I might not have otherwise. I called it my hidden curriculum.

It wasn't that I had a perfect role model when I was coming up because I didn't. My father was really a poor example of who you wanted to imitate. But I made it in spite of him. Because I made it, I wanted to help others make it. Coaching allowed me to do that. I was able to get closer to them and have a conversation with them that wasn't just typical teacher-student type conversations. I got to know them and their parents and they got to see how I wanted to give back. I've been looking back since college. I thought someone was going to wake me up and say, 'Hey, you're not supposed to be doing this!' I was a poor kid, coming up on general assistance and food stamps. But I was motivated to do this.

I have policemen, teachers, school administrators, professional players, and everything else you can think of, whom I've been able to work with as young kids. Probably 80 percent of them were coming from some pretty poor backgrounds. I hear it all the time: 'Coach, if it had not been for you, I might not have made it.''

Sports and coaching don't get the credit that they deserve, especially in inner-city neighborhoods. It's often put on the back burner in the name of education. But sports can make a kid study, do the right thing, and mature into a great citizen. It's at the top of my list when it comes to ways to connect to kids and get them on the right track. There are so many messages about life that you teach kids through sports. You lose a game and you still have to go and shake the other players' hands. On the street, you lose a game and you're ready to go up against somebody's head. In organized sports you learn self-control. You learn discipline. You learn how to take care of your body. You learn the limits of your body. You learn teamwork. And the list goes on and on.

Many people who have never played sports might not understand all of the lessons learned through sports. They might have to learn those same lessons in a number of other ways. But with sports, and with the right coaches, you can learn so much about life in one place.

I've been a principal and a deputy superintendent. I've had to help raise district test scores and school test scores. But sports is still a top motivator for children.

When the kids left me, they knew it meant going to college and getting an education. It didn't mean going on to play professional basketball or scoring 20 points. It was how can I use this talent to put myself in a better position than what my parents are in? I've had some who went on to play professionally, but I've had a whole lot more graduate college. That means just as much to me as the ones who made it to the NBA.

Don R. Pittman is a retired basketball coach from Chicago, Ill., where he coached for more than 25 years at schools such as South Shore High School and Carver High School. Now an associate professor at Northeastern Illinois University, Pittman remains a mentor for many former players and coaches in the Chicago area.

DUMB LUCK
CARL ARRIGALE

Coaching has always been in my blood. My dad coached CYO basketball. I was always part of a situation where there was always a kids' league. I grew up in a Catholic parish so there was always coaching going on. I thought it was something that I might be interested in doing but it was never a real definite. They would get the older kids involved. The seventh and eighth graders would coach the younger kids so they kind of brought you up in it a little bit. But when I went away to school, I was kind of out of it for a while. But just by dumb luck I ran into a high school rival and he told me he was going to be up for the local high school job where I grew up. We talked a little bit and he wasn't from the area so I told him that if he needed some help to let me know. We met a couple days later when it looked like he was going to get the job. So we decided that I was going to help him and that got me started. That was at St. John Neumann.

He only lasted a year. The next year they hired the JV coach and moved him up. We had become friendly so he hired me to stay on to help him. Then after about a four-year stint, he moved on and the job was open. I went for the job and has been there ever since.

My high school coach was a big influence on me, which is ironic because he's in our league now and we coach against each other. He came on my junior year and I learned a lot about what it took to put a team together, and the atmosphere you want to have around your team. I try to do that with my teams. I try to keep a family atmosphere. We preach family. I learned that from my grade school and high school experiences.

I came up in a situation where my grad school parish not only had the CYO teams but intramurals, girls on Saturdays, boys on Sundays and the families were all there after church. It was really a positive thing growing up. Everybody was part of the whole thing.

When I went to high school it was a little different. But my coach still made it an atmosphere where if someone was willing to do something for you, you were willing to do something for them. That's kind of the way we approach it now. We want to really be there for our guys. I coach in Catholic schools so I'm not doing it for the money. I probably lose money over the course of the year. It's a lot of family time and a lot of money but I'm putting kids in school and hopefully giving them positive experiences that they can pass on to their children and friends and families.

We try to play an unselfish brand of ball and let everybody know they are not above the team. We try to teach them values that you try to teach everybody else but sometimes through sports it's a little easier because it's something that they like and it's something they are willing to do. Without sounding too cliché, the sum is great than the parts. It's really simple, but it takes a lot of sacrifice to be successful in whatever you do. We've been consistent with a positive message.

In our city, there are so many schools now, all these public schools and charter schools going up. So a lot of kids are running from places if they don't like the message or don't want to be told or taught. And the parents are allowing it to happen. We've been fortunate. We've gotten good kids and they stay. That's why we've been able to be successful. At the end of the day, we're putting a lot of kids in college, getting an opportunity to further their education and play some basketball. That's the reward for me in the end.

Carl Arrigale has been built Neumann-Goretti High School in Philadelphia into a perennial basketball power as head coach over the past 16 years. He has led the team to 10 Philadelphia Catholic League Championships, three state titles and a regular ranking among the nation's top boy's high school programs.

BORN TO COACH
TRACY DILDY

I think I was born to coach.

Like everybody else I thought I would be playing in the pros after my career at University of Illinois-Chicago. But at the time of training camp, I ended up stretching some ligaments in my leg and I couldn't go to camps that I was invited to. My college coach, Bob Hallberg, saw that I was not in a good mood. So he was the one that presented it and said, come and stay and help him on the coaching staff.

Once I got involved in it, it kept me around the game that basically saved my life. It fell into place. The game of basketball kept me from hanging out with some of my other friends and getting in all types of trouble. Now I was able to stay around the game and make a living. The recruiting part came easy to me because I was the guy that recruits stayed with when they came to visit the campus. I've been blessed to be successful.

What it has also done is taught me a lot of discipline and strengthened my faith walk. I am a proud Christian and I kind of wear it on my sleeve. So it's been a great journey.

I'm not perfect. I'm a work in progress. I still struggle in certain areas. In this business, after a couple losses, it kind of put you in those areas that you struggle with. But one of the things that I try to take pride in is being an example. I don't preach anything that I don't practice. I try to have that as a forefront where these guys can see I am who I say I am. It's not just a front. It's not a hypocritical thing.

Most of my guys are from Illinois. They all know where I'm from. I'm from the inner city of Chicago, which is two miles from campus. So I am from what we would call the hood. So I am hooded in the hood. Some of my guys come from two-parent homes but most of them come from single-parent homes. Some have relationships with their dads and some don't. I tell them in the recruiting process that they are going to be told on a number of occasions, 'Hey, I love you!' That's not a phrase that a lot of African-American males are used to hearing coming from another male, especially one who is not related to them. We do practice, 'I love you.' And it's all right for me to love you.

I really preach family. Everything during the game we talk about how it relates to family. Once you become a part of our family, you're stuck with us for the rest of your life. It's not once you're done with your eligibility you're gone. You are stuff with us for the rest of your life. They see that when guys come back.

The guys are always free to come to my house. We do a lot of things together. We might watch a football game together and order food. My thing is we spend a lot of time together. We do a lot of off the court type, family type things together. We have rap sessions. We have people come in to do lifestyle things with our guys.

My whole message is share where I came from and share how I was raised with a single mom who raised five kids. Four of her five kids graduated from college. I always try to bring people who look like them in to see them. I'm a big believer that you can't be something you don't see. I really want to prepare my guys for life.

We must be doing something right. We have kids from the inner city and from the suburbs who never go home. And we don't have guys transfer from our program.

Every summer, we have guys that come back with families, working success, and doing great things in and outside of basketball. We love our success stories. That's why we do the life skills. We have over 8-10 speakers who come in to do a life skills session with our guys from lawyers to agents to teacher to other coaches to police officers. Our guys get to see that for me to make it, I don't have to have basketball. It really opens up their hope and expectations. It's no longer the thought that the only way I can make it is basketball.

Tracy Dildy is head men's basketball coach at Chicago State University, where he just completed his fourth season with the team. In 2013, he led the team to the school's first Division I conference championship in the Great West Conference. He previously coached at schools such as University of Illinois-Chicago, UAB, Ole Miss, and Auburn.

VALUE SUCCESS ON THE IMPACT
STEPHANIE WHITE

I have a picture from when my parents brought me home from the hospital my dad had me in one hand and a basketball in the other. So I don't remember a time in my life without basketball.

I finished playing at the professional level in 2003 and got into coaching right after that. I coached at the college level for four years and I think this is my eighth or ninth season coaching at the professional level. When I was playing in high school and college, I didn't think about coaching very much. I actually got lucky. My last year playing for the Indiana Fever, I got approached by a college coach at Ball State and was asked if I would be interested. At that time I said sure, why not? I might as well try it. I had injuries and I knew that my career was winding down. Then I loved it.

As a player my strengths were my understanding of the game, my work ethic and wanting to be best but also just naturally understanding what was happening on the court. I was able to see the game in a different way, almost with a coach's eye. So it was a natural transition. But the hardest part about the transition is realizing you don't have control anymore. I wasn't able to be out on the floor. But I loved the new challenge. I loved challenging my mind to think outside the box, the strategy involved when it comes to scouting, and trying to make your team better and utilizing your strengths and hiding your weaknesses. So it was a natural competitive transition but also a mental transition.

We're very lucky in Indiana to have great leadership in Tamika Catchings. She lives by example in terms of being a better person than a player. So that definitely helps. But the biggest thing for me is that I've been there to I understand the challenges that they're going through such as being ready every single day, the travel, making sure you're eating right, and when you're in a little bit of a slump from a confidence standpoint. Players want to take some ownership too. So I understand that. I understand where they're coming from. We have to have that open dialogue. It's not me and them, it's us. Having playing experience gives me respect from the players. And now having the coaching experience helps me communicate better with the players.

As you transition from college to the professional level, a lot of these players are used to eating whatever they want whenever they want or they had training table where everything is provided for them. You have to figure out how to eat right, how much time you need before and after the game to eat, what type of food you're eating so that you can best energize and fuel your body. Then after our season they go to Europe. If you've never been to Europe and you're trying to adapt to a new culture, food is a huge part of that. Usually it takes them a little while to get used to but it's certainly something that we talk about. They're on their own for the first time. There's no curfew. Nobody's telling them they can and can't do something. It's not as structured as college so we talk about all the things that they can do for an optimum performance. It's their life. You have a short window of opportunity to play basketball for a living. You want to do it for as long as you can. In order to do that, you have to take care of certain areas.

As a former player, you talk about life after playing basketball and let them know it's not going to be around forever. You have to manage your money, think about what else you're going to do and challenge your mind. We often have those conversations. There are some opportunities available through the league but I think we can still do a better job. As former players and some current coaches in the league, we're looking into a retired players association, something like the NBA has. We had our first meeting this fall. One of our main talking points was helping these ladies transition from playing to the real world, so to speak.

Whenever you are in a leadership role, whether it's coaching or teaching or running a company, life coaching is part of your mission. You always want to prepare your players, your teammates, and your co-workers for success. Part of the process involves understanding priorities, teaching responsibility, accountability, compassion, and giving back. All of those things are important. When it comes down to it, we always tell our players that some people aren't going to remember the stats that you had on the floor but they are going to remember the impact that you made in somebody's life and that's the most important thing.

Coaching is not for everybody. There are some players who say there is no way I can be a coach. But there are certain players you can just tell from their leadership style, the way they play the game, the way they communicate on the floor, that coaching is in their DNA. They might not know it yet. When one of your players approach you and say, 'Hey, I'd like to do that,' I give them a scouting report. I tell them I want you to do a scouting report on this team. I want you to give me every strength and weakness of the players on the floor. I want a game-plan on how we're going to defend their plays. I want a game-plan on how we're going to attack their defense. I just show them a little bit of what life as a coach would be like. Certainly we need more former players getting into coaching and we need the passion that they have for the game.

As a player, success was all about the wins and the championships, the scoreboard and all of those tangible things. Certainly as a coach, you're always held up against your record and your championships. But as I got older, my definition of success has changed a bit. I think that I would like to value my success on the impact that I have had on our players and the impact that you see going beyond the game. How successful are they in life? Are they prepared when they are finished playing to be citizens that impact the lives of others? As a league, have we given everything to make these players successful? Have we given everything we can to make this league successful? So why there are certainly tangible results that make you successful and unsuccessful, I think there are a lot of intangible results. I probably won't truly be able to measure that until I'm able to step away from the game and look at it from a different perspective.

I do have former players who contact me and ask my advice or see how I can help them get into their careers. One example, one of my former players at the University of Toledo wanted to get into broadcasting. I fell into broadcasting. I got lucky. When I was coaching in Chicago in the WNBA, the Big 10 Network was starting in Chicago. Now I do broadcasting in the winter and coaching in the summer. But this particular player emailed me when I started on the Big 10 Network. She was a senior in college at that point. She said I want to do what you are doing. I thought she wanted to coach but she said she wanted to get into TV. She asked what she needed to do and who she needed to contact. So I gave her some advice, she took it and started at the ground level. Now she's a sideline reporter for the Cleveland Cavaliers. Fortunately, I was able to give her a little bit of advice to get her started but the work ethic she had took her to another level. Now every time I run into her or we shoot each other texts, I am so proud. She made her dreams come true.

Stephanie White is an assistant coach with the Indiana Fever. After a stellar playing career that included a national championship at Purdue, National Player of the Year Award, and six years in the WNBA, White went on to coach at

Ball State, Kansas State and the University of Toledo before returning to the WNBA as a coach with the Chicago Sky and Fever. She also is a college basketball analyst with ESPN and the Big 10 Network.

SHOOTING UNDER THE MOONLIGHT
CORY ARNETT

Success means hard work. There is no success within putting in the necessary hard work that you need to get results.

From my childhood playing basketball and being that my dad was an NBA player, I was always around high level competition and players. I saw that it took hard work for them to be that way. I knew that if I wanted to succeed, I would have to do the same thing.

As a child, I was blessed to go out watch Magic Johnson and Larry Bird play in the championship out in Salt Lake City, Utah. Seeing those players and all the hoopla and attraction that everyone had toward them, they always talked about what they had to do behind closed doors to get there. They had to put in the hard work to hone their craft to be the type of players that they were. Of course we they changed the face of the game once they came into the NBA. But I remember that vividly. So I went back to California and started working hard to be the best player that I could be even at 10-11 years old at the time.

Back then no kid thought about going out of high school to the NBA. First, it was let's try to get to a D-I school. We knew we had to work hard to make it to one level then to work hard to make it to the next level. My dad would always tell me you have to continue to work hard. He would say while somebody else is home sleeping, you need to be on the court shooting under the moonlight. I heeded his message. I put in the time to raise the level of my game so I could be a top-notch player.

My dad was my first coach. He only coached me my first year playing in maybe the second grade. He would always give me tidbits here and there though. At the time, he was still playing so I was able to watch him and watch other players that he played with. So I picked up a lot of nuances from the game back then.

My favorite player was Kareem Abdul-Jabbar. I got a chance to go to one of his camps shortly after that national championship game. I fell in love with the 'Cap. I was also blessed to be a ball boy for the 1985 Lakers so I was always around him and that time. When they take the dunk out of the game because of you that means you're great.

Being able to share some of the knowledge that I've gained over the years is very important to me. We understand that each generation has its type of players. And now we have the worldwide web players and everything is about me, me, me. But if I'm able to share some of the tidbits and the fundamentals that have gotten away from the game, it helps. They realize that. A lot of the players that I train and coach want to know how it was when I played on a team with Clyde Drexler and played against Michael Jordan and things like that. They want to take what they can get and use it for themselves.

There's been a lot of players who reached that top level and things just didn't pan out. But to even get to that level takes a lot of work. You have to be dedicated. And for those who make it, they have to work even harder to stay there. So I tell people, be the first in the gym and the last to leave. Always be professional. Always be a team player. And then after all that, work some more.

Cory Arnett is former assistant coach for the Los Angeles Slam of the ABA and new head coach of the ABA team to debut in Indiana for the 2014-15 season. He is also a former professional player who had stints in the NBA, CBA and ABA. Arnett is CEO of Capiquis, a basketball training, player development and professional basketball consulting business.

THE HARDER YOU WORK, THE LUCKIER YOU GET
LEFTY DRIESELL

I never thought I would coach so long. I started out as a junior varsity coach at the school I attended from the second grade to the 12th in Norfolk, Virginia, Granby High School. When I got out of Duke, the first year I worked for Ford Motor Company. Then I went back to Granby as a junior varsity coach. The next year I got the varsity job Newport News High School. We won a lot of games over there. Then I got the Davidson job. When I was 30 I said I'm not going to be doing this when I'm 40. When I was 40 I said I'm not going to be doing this when I'm 50. When I was 50 I said I'm not going to be doing this when I'm 60. When I was 60 I said I wasn't going to be doing this when I'm 70. Well, I was still coaching after 70. It was something I enjoyed.

My first job I made $3,200 coaching at teaching at Granby High School. My first college job at Davidson I made $6,200. If I would have stayed in high school I would have made $6,400. When I went to Maryland, I made $20,000 and I was the highest paid coach in the ACC. It's never been about money for me. I just love it.

A lot of people think coaching is easy. But it's a tough job. It keeps you busy. It's something different every day. You're dealing with young people and that keeps you young. It's a different challenge all the time.

My definition of success is doing the best that you can do. Don't shortcut. I have a saying, the harder you work, the luckier you get. That's sort of my philosophy of success. I've never won a national championship, never been to the Final Four but I feel like I've been a success, in my mind anyway. I worked hard. I never took shortcuts. I helped others develop and learn some principles they could apply to other areas of their lives.

I tried to tell players to be the best that they can be. When they get up in the morning and their feet hit the ground, just do the best you can do. Be honest and be a good person. That's in the classroom, as a citizen, and as a basketball player. I try to be the best I can be every day.

I think every coach thinks of his team as family. Some groups I coached were better than others. We'd go to church together. They'd come over my house for dinner. Every good team does that. And I think faith is very important. We prayed before and after games. Like I tell everybody, nobody's gotten out of this world alive yet. So you better be ready when your time comes. You just share messages and you hope that they get it.

One of the benefits of coach is watching your players grow up and become successful. Some of my players are doctors. Some are lawyers. Some are coaches. Some are politicians. I've coached for so long. Just seeing them be successful, being happy, raising families, is gratifying.

Lefty Driesell is the only coach to win more than 100 games at four different colleges or universities. He coached at Davidson College, University of Maryland, James Madison University and Georgia State University. He retired in 2003 after coaching 41 years.

LEGACY BUILDS SUCCESS
JOEL HAWKINS

I never considered coaching a job. I enjoy kids. I guess it was predetermined. I remember very distinctly when I was in the third grade, a teacher asked me what I wanted to be when I grew up and I told her I wanted to be a basketball coach. And nothing I've seen since that time and I've had opportunities where I would have made a lot more money but I always wanted to be a coach.

I was a normal student. I'm from a large family and I'm the baby in my family, a family of 12. And all my brothers and sisters went to college. So it was already determined that I was going to college. Now what I wanted to be in college could be entirely different. I was an athlete in his school and when I got to perform creditably and people started showing some interest in me, I knew I knew then I wanted to be a coach because my coaches have been very close to me and I knew that somewhere down the line that would help me. I wanted to do the same thing to the kids I coached.

I remember when I was in the sixth grade, my oldest sister had graduated college and she taught me so I had to be the model student in my class. I had to go to band if I wanted to play ball, I had to be in the band and do something else. I played the trombone. Hated it! I couldn't wait til I got out of class but it taught me some mental discipline. I tried to carry that over with my family when I got married and had kids. I gave the boys a chance. They were good athletes but I gave them a chance to do something other than being a good athlete. I wanted them to be a part of the whole picture rather than just playing basketball. My dad was an uneducated man. He didn't have an education but he stressed that everybody in our family did. It was a kind of thing where we saw what each other were doing and the older ones and it makes you want to be successful. He always pointed to the fact that success was a part of hard work. I always did that.

Oddly enough, of the eight of us, only four of us played sports, my sister, who was a fantastic basketball player, two of my brothers and myself. We all played the same sports. My sister played softball and basketball and we played baseball and basketball. We learned a lot from that.

I was the baby. Everybody wanted to help me. They were very informative. They let me know how important hard work and work ethic were. And I was lucky enough to get a scholarship.

Character is what you are when no one is looking. If you're going to do something that is shady when no one is looking, that's you. That's your character. It's important that they understand that. I haven't saved all the kids that have come through me. But a lot of kids have told me that they are better citizens as a result of playing on my basketball teams.

What I really try to do is show (players). People may not believe what you say but they believe what you do. I was never late for practice. I always came to practice. Consequently, all of my kids came to practice. The only difference between a great basketball player and a good basketball player is his work ethic. If you outwork him, you're going to be better than he is. If he shoots 50, you shoot 150, if you want to be as good. With me it's show and tell. You don't have to tell me anything. Show me.

A lot of people asked me how my teams became so disciplined. I tell them the game is bigger than them and it's bigger than me. They played this game before we were here and they're going to play it after we are gone. I tried to steer them in that direction. I'm not a stark disciplinarian like some people think. I just teach the big picture and they get it.

Success is when you take someone with you to that pinnacle that you call success. And that might be different for everybody. When I was growing up and my family was pushing me to be successful, I believed that I was. The reason is because I thought I was the best that I could be. They were a lot of reason for that. My dad always stressed that. It doesn't matter what you do, son, as long as you do it the best that you can and you will have no regrets.

Joel Hawkins coached high school basketball for nearly 40 years at Southern Lab (Baton Rouge), Lake Providence and G.W. Griffin (Lake Providence) with a career record of 1,071-263. At Southern Lab, he won 11 state titles in a span on 13 years. In 2003, he coached LeBron James and Chris Paul in the Michael Jordan Classic. In March 2005, he became the all-time wins leader in Louisiana high school basketball history. He retired from coaching in 2007, the same year he was inducted into the Louisiana Sports Hall of Fame.

FAMILY AND SUCCESS GO HAND IN HAND
RICK INSELL

    Success has got to do with your work ethic. You've got to have a high moral standard. I think your kids have got to know that you care for them and your kids have got to know that you're fair. I think at that point you're gonna have success. We've won a lot of basketball games and I know in some people's eyes making a lot of money really exemplifies their success. But as far as my family being close and being able to go places they we've wanted to go… If it had not been for my success on the basketball court, I couldn't do anything without my family around. There isn't a place around this country that we haven't been. The only reason that we've been able to go those places is because of the game of basketball.

    A lot of people I hear, my friends, and I hear other people on TV when they're glad when their kids get grown and they go off on their own. My family enjoys being around each other. My sons enjoy being around me and I enjoy being around them and my wife is part of it. Even though she might go shopping and not go to the games she's still part of it after the games and when we all get together to talk about what's going on during the game or during the term or whatever, she's there. It's meant my whole life. I don't know if you could put a price on that or not. Did I think that was what I was getting into when I got into coaching? No. I didn't even have any idea. But when you are able to play in New York and you are able to take your wife and kids, and you're able to go to Ellis Island, Empire State Building, and places like that that they were able to experience when they were the age in junior high and they were able to say that they've been to Washington, D.C., to the Smithsonian and saw all the monuments there. And it's all because of the game of basketball. We've been to almost all the major cities and it's all because of the game and our success. I could never put a price on that.

When I first got into coach, the first meeting I went to was a Quarterbacks Club meeting. That was a support group, they called it the Quarterbacks Club, but it supported all of the other sports at the high school as well. I can remember someone saying if you win four games we're going to nominate you for coach of the year. So you know that was my very first goal. I wanted to show them by Christmas we're gonna win four games. Did I know anything about the people we would be playing, the competitors? No. I knew nothing about conference, or my own team. But I knew one thing... I wanted to win four games before Christmas. I guess at that point I began to set goals. We were able to win four games before Christmas and have a successful season right at the beginning. Then we were able to go far in the tournament. I guess at that point the burn inside the individual takes over. Did I ever dream the things that would happen and that would materialize for us would take place when I took the job? Absolutely not. Never once crossed my mind. Never once motivated me to do anything. I just coached. I just enjoyed going out there in the afternoon working with the young ladies, giving it my all and seeing them give it their all and scheduling the toughest competition in America. We were one of the first teams that started traveling in 1984-85, one of the first high school teams. There were a few of us but not that many, especially on the girls' side of things. We went to Altoona, Pa., and they were ranked No. 1 in the country and we ended up at No. 2 in USAToday that year. They didn't have any games left to play and our association would not allow us to play any more after we got through with our state tournaments. The following year, we scheduled a game and we went to Altoona and won that tournament. At that point is when we really started traveling around the country.

I think your players gravitate to you. If they see how intense, how focused and how hard you work, they're going to work hard. If they see you with a nonchalant attitude and you're not self-disciplined… You can't fool dogs and you can't fool kids. Can't do it. They see very quickly if you are serious and if you're focused. I'm a very disciplined individual. Not just with myself but I'm a disciplinarian. It's all business when you step across the line. My players have taken on that within themselves also. If all we've ever taught you about the game of basketball is Xs and Os, then we've failed because there's a lot more to it than that. Basketball is like the game of life. Somewhere along the way, you're gonna have to learn how to compete. You've got to use this as a learning process, to grow up. Sure it's great to win and it's great to play in big games and we have a great time. But it's being able to do what you have to do at the right time. We talk about that every single day. When you step across the line, you have to be ready to go.

The last time I checked, in the game of basketball, it took five players. My teams are my family. I've had girls who played for me whose mothers I coached. That's says a lot for yourself and for your program when you have mothers who want their children to be involved in what they were involved in. That says a lot about your success. There were times when we didn't know how many games we'd won. We didn't know. We never talked about it, we never worried about it. We were together and we were doing what we enjoyed doing.

Rick Insell is in his ninth year as head women's basketball coach at Middle Tennessee State University, where he is the school's all-time winningest coach.

His winning percentage ranks in the top 10 among active coaches. Insell started his coaching career at Shelbyville (TN) Central High School where he guided the Golden Eaglettes to a record 10 state championships and two USA Today national championships (1989, 1991).

WINDOW INTO THE WORLD
POKEY CHATMAN

    A lot of coaches will tell you that success is measured on so many different levels that aren't always witnessed from people on the outside. They can never really measure the true growth of the players and the people and the staff that are involved day to day. We know, as coaches, how we are judged by the wins and loss columns but there are so many wins and losses that never get seen. There are so many successes for players and for coaches and eventually that evolves into the big group and the team.

    I'll say this. I think I was a perfect age. I call myself a Title IX kid in terms of being able to have a front row seat and an active participant in some of the things that came down the line. For me, I played for Sue Gunter, then I went to work for her. So I had a front row seat to the grind. I remember Sue tells the story of her big coaching job when she took the job at Stephen F. Austin and she made $6,500 a year and she thought she hit the lottery. The point of that was the money doesn't change the great ones. They have the work ethic and the process of doing things.

    Being the age that I was and working with Coach Gunter, she never had any help. She was always the bus driver, the coach, the trainer… She was everything. Being able to work with her at an early age, I was able to have a lot on my plate and fortunately was able to handle that. In three years I probably got seven or eight years of experience. What that translates to is we don't have one dimension players and it was impossible for me to be a one dimensional coach. Some of the things that I lived and went through I can tell a closely related story to my players or I don't have to tell a story. They can just look at it. All of those things kind of go into the pot to make something special, not just with your team that's on the court but with your extended team and your staff. I have a lot of things like that I can draw from.

There are so many levels. When you are in the pros, there is the basketball side, there's the business side, there's the branding side, there's the 'your shelf live is 'X' amount of years you need to get it done' side. That changed as my level and my coaching changed, from LSU to Europe to over here in the professional level. I think transparency is good in terms of they need a window into the world because this is the closest step they get to the real world and how things operate. These players go overseas in Europe. That's not the real world. There's no business model over there. Two players on the team make over $800,000 and one makes $1 million. It's even more so to be real and transparent in terms of what's going on and how it's going on. Obviously on the business side, there are things they can't know but I think it's always important to let them get a peek inside the real world of things.

I never imagined growing up that I could participate in the game I loved and get paid to do it. One, my payment was getting an education at LSU. Then you're going to pay me to coach somebody? It's just not something that's on the list of things to do and be when you were my age. I just love what I do. I don't think the passion is different. I think maybe I've gotten a better perspective of things, hopefully, after 22 years of coaching. I'm just a fanatic. One of the best days of the year for me, beside it being Christmas Day for obvious reasons, is all of those basketball games that were on TV that day. We do our Christmas Christmas Eve. I remember my sister came into my living room and she said, 'Are you serious? Are you working today?' I said, 'No! I'm not working. It's KD and the Thunder run a triple drag. I gotta get clips for Elena.' I say that because I love it. I love what I do so I don't feel like I'm working.

When you watch a game, there's always a game within a game. The same goes true with teams. There's always the play within the play or the players within the team that you see that meteoric growth that maybe is not recognizable to the outside world. One particular player for me was Courtney Vandersloot. She came in here from a mid-major. I had a veteran in front of her. That veteran was injured the first year and she was thrown into the fire. The second year the same thing happened with Ticha Penicheiro and it was a really, really close call of her sinking but then she started swimming. To see that growth and that leadership and being vocal and being my toughest player was amazing. At one point she had taken 19 charges and only committed one. I'm just using that one example but there are so many things. I'm watching Elena Delle Donne who for three years played position 5 at Delaware and she comes to me and within the first 13 days of being on my team I put her at 3 different positions. It's always things like that within the confines of the game that I love.

But when I have to take a step back and try to get away, I'm a jazz enthusiast. It's the best. It's the one thing that helps me slow down because you have a million things going. It's February and I'm thinking about my first seven practices and practicing the dribble handoff. You might get a kid that's a really good player but they were never taught what to do in a dribble handoff. So you start getting excited about all of that and that brings it back to basketball.

On the men's side they play 82 games. We play 34. But two of my opponents on my side I play five times. So it's the nuances. It's not going to be any magical plays. It's going to be players making plays, fundamentals, little tweaks after timeouts, all the little nuances like that where you kind of steal about eight possessions a game because so many games for us come down to one or two possessions. That was new for me. All the years in college you're playing people twice. You're playing somebody five times in 3½-4 months. After my players are done playing for me, I want them to be able to recognize the things that might not be recognizable to the naked eye and only because they were in my program, in terms of the communication, in terms of the growth, in terms of the progress. I think the easiest time to do that is when you're on the court. But when you're off the court, it's the locker room, the tough times. I want them to be able to say, 'She was always present' and I'm not just talking about during the game. I had a staff meeting this morning at 7:30. Courtney Vandersloot was playing against Diana Taurasi's team, Sue Bird's team, and that delayed my staff meeting because we tuned in. And when that game was over I wanted 'Sloot' to know, hey, you may be 3,000 miles away but we're present. I always talk to them about being present and being in the moment and giving them ownership of things. I think when they come back they'll see that I'm still doing that but hopefully I'm a little better at it and still building young ladies into strong human beings.

Dana 'Pokey' Chatman is general manager and head coach of the Chicago Sky of the WNBA. After her playing career at LSU, she stayed at the school as an assistant coach and later took over the helm from her coach and mentor, Sue Gunter. Her career includes several coach of the year awards and three consecutive trips to the Final Four and three championships in Moscow.

STAND FOR SOMETHING
MIKE KAYES

I played basketball my whole life. I love the game and I love working with kids through sports. I helped start Stewards of the Game and our motto is to teach life lessons through sports. I grew up in a small town in upstate New York and there wasn't much else to do but play sports. Most of the lessons I learned about perseverance, hard work and teamwork, just finding out how tough you were and dealing with it, mostly came from sports and good coaching I had as a kid. So it's always wanted to give that back to my kids and other kids I coach. I think through sports you can really teach kids some wonderful lessons just about growing up and how to handle situations. I think it's unique because there is so much emotion in sports you can really have kids' attention and you can really teach some really good things.

I think the first lessons I had was from my Pop Warner football coach when I was in probably fifth or sixth grade. I remember my coach telling us on the first play of the game, no matter how big the guy is on the other side of you, you hit him as hard as you can. And it just gave you the confidence that by setting the tone, playing aggressive as you can from the get go sent a message to the other team and also to your teammates that you were ready to play. So I've always believed that you gotta be ready to play emotional and physically and you gotta give it your best effort right from the start. I try to get my kids prepared to hit the ground and send a message to the other team early that you are ready to play 60 minutes or however long the game is. I think being prepared and having intensity from the start really sets the tone, especially if your opponent comes out a little flat or if you're in front of a hostile crowd, it can take the crowd right out of it. That's one lesson I learned early from that particular coach.

    I played sports since I was real young. I played a lot of different sports. I've had some success and some failure. I've probably learned more from the defeats that I've had as a player or coach than I've had from victories. I remember in high school playing basketball listening to the national anthem and I would be nervous. I'd look over to my dad and he'd wink at me. The message he was sending me was win or lose the game goes on, the country goes on and life is not gonna end if you don't win a particular game. So keeping in perspective winning and losing is very important so I try not to let my kids get too serious about the outcome of the game but I try to reward effort as much as the outcome of the game or the score. I always teach kids that if you try your best and give a good effort it doesn't matter what the score is. You are a winner. That's what Stewards of the Game tried to do with kids and that's what I try to do with coaching. I think the score can reflect so many things that are out of your control as a player or coach. So all you want your kids to do is give their best effort. And that's really the key to youth sports.

    My friend and I got tired of what we were seeing, some of the cut throat competition, win at all costs and stacking teams, parents and coaches swearing and the referees, just the ugly side of sports that many of had heard about. We decided we would take a fresh approach and we're both Christians and we wanted to share our faith with the kids in sports. We wanted to teach values and focus on good fundamentals and building up the total kid and not just what is your win-loss record at the end of the season. We're competitive and we try to win but we try to keep it in perspective.

    It's been fantastic. We've grown by leaps and bounds. We've done a lot of things that a lot of kids had never had the opportunity of doing.

In any situation or league, if you a good coach you tend to have a good experience. If you have a bad coach, you have a bad experience. What we're trying to do is create the total atmosphere, the total philosophy of what we're trying to do with sports. Every coach buys into what we're trying to do in terms of stressing values and fundamentals and teamwork and fair play and sportsmanship. If you are not consistent, kids will watch what you do as much as they listen to what you say. You've got to be consistent with your message so we talk a lot about not just talking the talk but walking the walk. We do that at a coach's level, and administrative level, and all aspects of what we're trying to do. That's really the only way to build a program or a tradition. Stand for something consistently. When you think of any successful program and you think of what they represent, Indiana Hoosiers and UCLA in times past, they stand for something and I want us to stand for something.

Mike Kayes served as athletic director and head basketball coach at the Community School of Davidson in Davidson, NC. He is co-founder of the youth sports ministry called Stewards of the Game and also author of the book Coaching Youth Basketball with Faith and Fundamentals.

PARENTING A PROGRAM
RAY LOKAR

There's a story I often share. I had been away from the school for quite some time and the players didn't really know me so I had to spend some time earning their trust and respect. We had a really good player named Jonathan Haywood and he ultimately got a scholarship to go to Loyola Marymount. I knew he was really really talented. We were walking through our gymnasium hall of fame one day and we were looking at all the retired uniforms. We had a big football tradition at Bishop Amat. No basketball jerseys in the trophy case. So I asked John. Do you know how you get your uniform up in the trophy case? He said set some kind of a record? I said no. Our criteria, here at Amat, is that you have to be the player of the year in our section. He said, "Oh." So I said do you know how you become player of the year? He said lead the section in scoring. I said no. You have to be the most valuable player on the championship team. About 10 seconds went by and he smiled. Then he understood it wasn't about individual achievements or setting a record or leading the team in scoring. It's about leading my team to success. Ten months later, we won our section championship, he was the CIF player of the year because he was clearly our best player, and we retired his jersey. Now it's sitting in our hall of fame. At that point he realized it wasn't all about me and what I do. I'm going get my recognition by our team's success. If he had had the same statistics and we didn't win it all he probably wouldn't have been player of the year and his jersey probably wouldn't be in our gym. He realized what teamwork was all about. That kind of underlines the whole teamwork aspect.

Raising your son is big in trying to put together what is important to you because you have to pass that on. There are really two types of dads that coach and one is the one that is going to let their kid get away with everything and is only worried about their son and daughter's personal glory and making them look good. We've always tried to do the right thing because it's the right thing to do not because dad said so. It wasn't any different playing sports. We spent a lot of time talking about team and how to get everybody else in the mix. 12 years I coached my son in basketball. You really have to watch your Ps and Qs. They're watching you all the time, the example you set and what you say to everybody.

Now my entire coaching philosophy is we try to parent a program. We try to parent all the kids in the program. We spend a lot of time on things off the floor as well. We want them being good people, representing the community and representing the school. I just try to father all of those kids and get a lot of support from their parents too.

I remember when I first coached my son and it was scary because I didn't know what category I was going to fall in. So I really went out of my way. I was probably on him more and used him as an example. He knew that going in. I told him he would have to be better than everyone else or I'm going to have to let that other person play that position if you're not. I did that with baseball too. You can't pitch and play shortstop unless you're better than everybody else. You're not just going to be there because you're my son. A lot of coaches do that. We had a rule we wouldn't talk about the game once I left the driveway after the game, unless he brought it up. And he often did. I didn't want to be coach-dad. There were times I sat in the parking lot a long time before I pulled out because I got to decide when we left. But once we left, it was all on him. It was a good rule we had in our family, even with my daughters. Me and my daughter had a sign. If take was getting too tough like I got with her brother sometimes, she'd just pat her head. And she only had to do that once or twice. I think when you are coaching your own kids, you have to walk that fine line between being too lenient and being too tough, too hard on them. All of the other players knew that they weren't going to get disciplined any more than my own child would. That made for a pretty good relationship among the youth sports people. We tried to carry that through with all of my teams.

Ray Lokar has more than 30 years of experience as a youth basketball coach. He currently coaches at Fairmont Prep Academy. He led Bishop Amat High School to the 2002 California state championship and is a former president of the Southern California Interscholastic Basketball Coaches Association. Lokar also coached St. Anthony High School and Western Christian High School.

BIG GAME PHILOSOPHY
PETE POMPEY

Key to success: The ability to make youngsters to understand what you want them to do. Amazingly enough I've been successful in making young people understand what they need to do to be successful, which is not the easiest thing in the world. I would say it's a blessing to be able to get those things across to them. It's a common ground that I've seen with the basketball and football teams that I coached. It takes a while but it seemingly gets there.

How good you feel about yourself and how good you feel about the things that you've done, what kind of team success and team pride, and the levels that you reach based on the kind of work you put in it, and I really feel that it's the common thing… you only get out of it what you put in it. I've been fortunate enough to have had a lot of youngsters, I believe, to put a lot into it, all they had, and really felt good about what they've added to.

There have been some difficult times in my life and in my time of coaching and some of the things that are not related that may affect the coaching. But amazingly I've never wavered on the fact that this is what I wanted to do because I love doing it and the fact that I felt I could make some changes in some folks' lives, particularly youngsters, by being a part of this. So I couldn't walk away. There is someone who had an impact on me in the same respect when I was coming through high school and college. I never saw a twinkle in any of those guys to give up either. They worked hard and stuck with it. That's the way I wanted to be. We don't get to all the youngsters. We see some tragedies and we see some things happen to our kids. But that fortunately is the minority and not the majority. The majority of the kids have come along and took the word and took the training and the leadership and taken off with it.

They've stayed real focused. Even listening to them now, coming back 10, 15, 20 years later saying how much they appreciated what was done for them in whatever program they were in that I was in charge of.

When I went to high school, my first coach was William Mack Payne at Douglas High School. And Roy Craigway was there. Those two guys really influenced me. Then when I went to college, I had the great fortune of playing for two of the greatest coaches on the college level ever in Eddie Hurt at Morgan State University and then after Coach Hurt came Earl Banks, who was equally as strong and as important in the things that I believe in and the things that I set philosophies on.

When I left Edmondson High School and went to Dunbar and the national championship power program, it was a difficult situation going into that. The thing that really made me start to wonder about it a little bit was some of the people that I ran into. Kids were not used to something new and the change in their life. Sam Cassell, for instance, was one of them. That was one of the toughest acts I had to get around and bringing Sam around to my way of doing things and my philosophy. It was a very difficult one. At the same time, he was the leader of the basketball team that was coming off a very good year and I think Sam wanted to do things his way. He and I battled a little bit verbally and philosophically but in the long run, everything came together and we were successful together. He and I are good friends. I respect him a great deal and I think he feels the same way. He has moved on and been very successful with some of the things that I tried to instill in him and some of the things that Bob Wade tried to instill in him before me. But it was a difficult situation because he was not a guy that accepted change easy. But we got thru it and I was very proud of that moment in there.

There was another young man who was a basketball player.

Well, he felt he was a basketball player and I thought that he probably would have fit better as a football player at Edmonson. It took me a long time to make him see that he would probably be a better football player. His name was Warren Powers, just as an example. He was about 6-foot-6 and about 235 pound, as one of the coaches use to say, he was a long drink of water. But he was not a basketball player. He was basketball player size but he was more of a football player because he was a very physical guy and had that mentality. Warren came out for football after I talked him into it. He became a tremendous player. He still played basketball at the same time but he started to re-focus himself to football and he earned a scholarship to the University of Maryland, went on to play at Maryland for four years under Bobby Ross and Ralph Friedgen. He got drafted by the Denver Broncos and played there for five years and then played another four or five years with the Rams. So it was a success story, hoping and feeling like I had a little bit to do with it.

I know this is a cliché, but we work real hard trying to make youngsters understand your academics if your most important reason why you're here. You can use that as a springboard or a cushion in case other things don't work out. One thing about it is they can't take that from you. Your education and the things you do in the classroom, the way you get yourself prepared professionally in the academic world will carry you a long, long way. Football is only promised to a very few and basketball is the same way. You're not going to get rich off of it. Maybe 1 in 10,000 kids who participates in athletics may step onto a professional field or professional court. You have to have some strong basis to fall back on or to rely on. My feeling is always that the first base you want to look at because that will be there when all else is gone. It's worked over the years for the most part because we've had kids accept the idea of getting into the classroom even they may have had some difficulties along the way or some non-focused areas where they didn't think that was the most important thing. But I was able to change some of their thinking around and keep them focused and out of trouble and in the right frame of mind in terms of having the right focus.

Football and basketball are the same in that you are only gonna be as strong as the weakest man on there. If you are not on the same page and the same accord and the work level is not the same then you're going to have a weakness. Those spots are going to become serious disadvantages to you as you go along. I think that the one that kids started to realize and get under control a long time ago is that we have to be together and we want to be together. We can be on the same accord as to what our common goal is and I believe we can get it done together.

When you have a Sam Cassell that was the first one I knew it was a little more difficult. But the later Sam makes it a little easier because he is such a great leader and a great player everybody wants to follow, it just make the cohesiveness a tremendous asset.

But it takes work. And everybody has to work hard. Once they refocus themselves, it makes all the difference. Speaking about (the 1992 national championship team that included) Michael Lloyd, Donta Bright, Keith Booth, Cyrus Jones and Paul Banks... those kids were collectively one of the most together teams that Dunbar ever had in my eyesight. I'm sure there were others. But to have that much individual talent and to be able to use it in the team concept was really awesome. We went 29-0 and won a national championship. It was an incredible feat because we really didn't have real big kids. Bright and Booth were 6-5 and that basically was our size. But the heart of those kids, in particular, couldn't be measured until you saw them in a big game. And when you're heading for an undefeated season and a national championship, all of them are big.

I've never heard a youngster that I've ever coached say he didn't do anything from me or I don't appreciate our relationship. The thing about it is, I think, that most of them can walk away from it saying they got something out of this relationship. I think they can say, I got something out of him. He made my life better. He taught me the things that I should be focused on and the things that I should be doing to exist in this very complicated world.

Pete Pompey coached basketball and football nearly 40 years in Baltimore before retiring. He coached the Dunbar High School boys' basketball team to a perfect 29-0 record in 1992 and the national championship.

LOVE, RESPECT AND EDUCATION
RON 'FANG' MITCHELL

At the time I got into coaching, I was an entrepreneur. I had three sporting goods stores called Mr. Fang's Athletic Attire. Coaching really wasn't one of the things I had on my agenda. Opening sporting goods stores and managing retail stores was something that I was involved in. But I was helping out the coach for free at Gloucester County College where I played undergrad and the coach got sick. Since I was there and I played there, I said why not give it a shot.

Coaching is a tough job because of the fact that things are just changing so much whereas in days of old the respect factor is where we're running into a lot of problems. Because of that, it's just tougher to educate the young people. I've always said anyone that was associated with me at Coppin, that left out of here, if I could just get them to respect authority, by the time they left there, I think that would be half the battle for them to be successful in life. That's something that's just becoming so difficult. I have a mentoring group that's called Fang's Gang Institute. On our shirt we have Love, Respect and Education. Today it just becomes a battle with people.

It's enjoyable when you get the right kids. We're in a different situation here at Coppin because we don't have a lot of money. Sometimes I really get the problem kids. It just becomes difficult. So sometimes I have to start all over. I try to get a hold of kids that are going to have good character and good morals and want the opportunity just to be able to do the things to be successful in life.

I've always say them, especially coming out of the inner cities where I've gotten a lot of them, rights and wrongs in the ghetto are entirely different than the rights and wrongs in the Bible. I always felt that it's the Bible that I'm dealing with on the rights and wrongs.

That is a misconception to a lot of them. What is right to do? In the inner city, they might say it's all right to beat somebody when I know that is not the way it should be. But the whole fact of short cutting things or trying to have an attitude like that affects the game of basketball. It's going to affect it because there always going to look for a shortcut.

The thing I think is most difficult is when they try to change who you are and what you represent. That's the battle. I think it's always been a shortage of role models. I am a person that came out of the inner city. I had to work to get through school. I had to work really to get to where I am as a coach and a director of athletics. I do know that I worked at it the right way. I did it honestly. I didn't hurt anybody to get ahead. I haven't been money-driven or money motivated. Even when you see the situation when you are successful, you jump out of here because someone can always buy you. I didn't need to be bought and I wouldn't be bought. The inner city kid who needed that help, who needed that opportunity, I felt like I could do something for them. I felt like I could be there to be able to talk to them about what is important in life. You need a proper balance in life. A lot of these kids don't understand that. That's why they're fighting in class and on the basketball court. That's why I say you need a balance to be successful in life and that includes spiritually.

I think the kids recognize that I'm a no nonsense person and that I want one or two things a certain way. I'm fighting them on how they wear their hair, how they wear their hats, things of that nature. I look at that as problems and all kinds of things that would affect them in moving forward in their life. It becomes a situation where there are so many little things now you start to not even be able to worry about what they do in the dorms, what they wear and things like that. I look at things like how do I go get a job if my hair is a certain way, if I'm dressed a certain way. Those are the things that I talk to them about but it becomes a battle.

I try to teach my players a certain way but then you look on television and you see the superstars doing the same thing. The difference is they made it. They can do certain things once they've made it. Kids don't recognize that.

All of them think they are going to the NBA. What makes it worse, even the walk-ons. I don't even discuss them going to the NBA. Some stuff you just don't need to talk about. But what I say is that you need to make sure you're covered in life. What are you trying to what your life? Ok. You're here and your purpose is to get an education where you can go out and make money, support your family and go out and be a positive contributor to society. That's what you're here for. You're using athletics as a vehicle to achieve these things. A lot of times they just don't want to hear that. But that's my job to try and make them understand how important a degree is. And then I have to teach them to work.

The work ethic is off. People don't work as hard as they used to in days past. A lot of people feel they are owed something. They feel like if they are going to get to the NBA it's just going to happen rather than working through it.

We are in a unique situation at Coppin. We always felt really proud because of the fact that we are a historically Black school, which really had nothing. So we really had no reason to be battling people. We didn't have the tools to be able to do it. But we had a lot of heart and a lot of desire and that's sometimes overcome that talent level. We were fortunate in the past. But I was also fortunate to get those types of kids that were hungry.

I think the thing that has always been a driving point and a selling point for historically Black schools is an opportunity and they've always been there for people as opportunities. When we get them, we get an opportunity to play against these so-called big schools, it's still an opportunity to prove that you can be successful against them. The students recognize what they can get from the bigger schools compared to what historically Black schools get. But it's a thing of pride. If you get the right, he's just going to work hard to be the best that he can be. It becomes more of a challenge to them if they have pride in themselves. We were very fortunate to have the opportunities to beat some of these schools. Those are the things that our kids will never forget. We've given them the opportunity but they've wanted the opportunity. Success has come through that.

To me, success doesn't have to be measured in dollars. But to me, success is going out and putting out the effort and doing the best possible job that you can and understanding where you're trying to go. Sometimes success to me was losing the game when we played as hard as we can and we did the best that we could. So it's gotta be in you that you know you've done the best that you can and you just keep knocking on the door and deal with it in that manner. Even when you lose, you can be successful. There are always opportunities to be successful. When you deal with life, that's ongoing.

I feel that I have achieved some levels of success. Even though I know that I have accomplished some things, I know there is still fight in me to accomplish more things. But if I can help people along the way, then to me that's success. When I look back at my life in that area, I hope that did well and that I'll have more opportunities to be successful.

Ron 'Fang' Mitchell has spent the last 27 years as the head men's basketball coach at Coppin State University in Baltimore, where he has lead the team to 10 Mid-Eastern Athletic Conference championships, six MEAC Coach of the Year Awards, and four appearances in the NCAA tournament, including a 1997 upset of No. 2 South Carolina in the NCAA tournament. Mitchell has won more than 600 games at Coppin State and Gloucester County College.

MY DOOR IS ALWAYS OPEN
DICK BENNETT

Since I retired it's become pretty much everything. You begin your coaching career or even playing career where your family is central and you make decisions based on raising a family then you get caught up in your profession, as I did for 35 plus years. But then as you finish, then the family becomes everything again. But at no time during my career did I ever try to do anything that would have a negative impact on our family. All of my decisions to change jobs or to move up were always considered with the family in mind and what would be best for them.

Sports was a huge part of everything I did. I moved from Pittsburgh, Pennsylvania, when I was about nine to Wisconsin and I can remember my father was always a great sports enthusiast. Throughout that time and throughout my athletic career, it was always whatever was in season. We played baseball, basketball and football. I actually did that all the way through college. There was not any degree of specialization. It was just the general love of the sport, of the competition of the camaraderie. It became almost like a surrogate family. The teams you played on were kind of secondary families.

Thankfully my wife was very much supportive of everything I did. The kids, because I coached high school ball for 11 years, were always important to our family and even to our little ones who were growing up. We had the players over to the house often. Our little ones were always included. They were at the gym. Our daughters were little cheerleaders and stuff like that. Our lives were connected to the youngsters we coached, probably moreso (as crazy as it might sound) when I started coaching collegiately. Then we became a second family to a lot of players, particularly in the early years when I was at the University of Wisconsin-Stevens Point and at Green Bay. The kids became a part of our family and I think my wife and my children enjoyed that role.

I remember always saying to them that no matter what goes on between the lines in practices and games, no matter how intense the setting is, no matter how much criticism you receive, no matter how good or bad our season is going, first of all my door is always open and you are always welcomed in our home. That was always true at any time, but especially during the holidays if guys couldn't get home. We would invite them to our place and sometimes it was hard for them to draw the line. I was a very intense coach and I was hard on players and demanded a lot. Sometimes it was hard for them to perhaps consider that other side. But as time has worn on and players had indicated to me the things that they had appreciated, that always come up, that they always felt welcomed and that they knew they had a place they could go.

My views might differ from many because I was always involved in rebuilding programs, almost from the beginning. The high schools that and all of the universities were in need of some restructuring and definite rebuilding. It was always my initial goal to become successful as soon as possible. That doesn't always mean you're going to be winning championships right out of the gate. Once a program or a team sees that it can compete, that in their eyes and in the eyes of those around the program, whether it be the community around them or the administration that hired you, or the media who covers you, that was regarded as success. Unfortunately, for myself, I always had a little higher standard. When people would say, 'Well, you had a successful season,' it was hard for me to accept that because I tended to remember the bad game or the last lost or so on. But as I gained more experience in the rebuilding process, and

I realized that it's going to take two or three years to get this program to the point where we can legitimate compete with the best teams at our level, I began to appreciate the effort and the performances of those teams that we kind of the foundation. So my views now of success have been sweetened a bit. It usually took about three years. But then the years four, five and beyond had a number of championships and outstanding accomplishments. That was a genuine thrill.

You have to have character to be able to build something. To me, being a part of something bigger than himself that is built on good and sound principles is all about character. I think character is one of those intangibles that would allow one to get by in almost any circumstance. It can keep you humble when things are going well and can enable you to show some pride when things are not going so well.

If there's been a defining characteristic of my teams and I think my own children is that they've been very hard workers, very dedicated to the task at hand. Often my teams were described as overachievers. I don't know if they were but they always carried on with an attitude and a work ethic that went beyond the ordinary. I also think humility is a characteristic I really tried to immolate and teach to our own children and our teams. We knew who we were and we didn't regard ourselves as being better than anyone and we felt very privileged to have the opportunities that we had.

There have been so many who might not have enjoyed outstanding success on the court but just the fact that they hung in there and finished the job when it might have been easier to go the other way. Probably the most spectacular example… I don't want to really mention my son, who I am very proud of who went on to play three years in the NBA and would have played a lot longer had his knees not failed him… is Terry Porter. Terry was not an outstanding high school player. He was not the best player on his team and was not recruited. We saw him early and got him when I was coaching at Stevens Point. He was pretty much an average student but he had a good heart. He had character. He had something that we thought we saw early. We were able to capitalize on that. He didn't even play his freshman year. He averaged less than one minute a game. But each year he grew because of his hunger, because of his character, his willingness to be instructed and he stayed humble through it all. He was of course drafted, had a 17-year career in the NBA and now he's a professional basketball coach in the NBA. Just watching him grow as a person and as an athlete was special. He was a person with character, who came from very humble beginnings and made it in the NBA. He never forget the people he came through with. He never forget his coaches, the players he played with… even his high school teammates. He appreciated everyone and treated them like family. Watching him remain the same person when he was in college has been most inspiring.

Dick Bennett coached for 28 seasons and won 316 combined games while at the helm of UW-Stevens Point, Green Bay, Wisconsin and Washington State. His teams appeared in six NCAA Tournaments at the Division I level. Bennett serves as a 2013-14 advisor to University of Wisconsin-Green Bay's head coach Brian Wardle, at the school Bennett spent 10 years building into a mid-major power. The school named a gymnasium in Bennett's honor.

BUILDING TEAMWORK
JAMES KAHN

When you hear the word teamwork, you think of sports right away. But teamwork starts way back in family, workplace and every other facet of life. People who are success, there's always cooperation among the members. It's not really just sports. You learn at a young age, and it's instilled in you, it really helps when you are growing up.

I'm sure a lot of what I learned was in the family structure, the working together. The family always had to pull together. Then when we started to play sports, teamwork was always stressed. You could see the importance when everybody pulled together things got accomplished a lot better.

I think back with my earliest experiences with little league baseball or basketball. You think at the time it's only important what you do until it's instilled in you by coaches that you are not the only spoke in the wheel, so to speak. I remember even my father coaching me for a while in basketball. He had to knock me down a few pegs when I thought I was more important than the rest of the team. In my experience, it was hard playing for my dad… for him and for me. You see a lot of problems today with parents. In my opinion, my dad bent over backwards to show everybody there was no favoritism. Sometimes I felt suffered in the other direction whereas sometimes today you see people being push by their parents too hard. My father made me work extra hard just so I could get the playing time.

One of the things that helped us be successful is that we were able to create a family atmosphere. I can go back. The first three years were kind of rough. Obviously success helps to breed the family atmosphere, but we did some things to bring us closer. We tried to do some trips and do some other things that would bring us together other than basketball. I think that was very helpful in making everybody come together. When you are in a group, whether it's family, or a job, not everyone is going to get along. But the more you do to get people to respect one another, it can really lead to success.

It's a funny situation. Everybody's different. Some are good leaders. Some don't speak at all. They lead by example. They lead by what they do. Some are vocal. You just get those leaders to set a good example for the rest of the team. Most times it was the seniors or the older players. Other times, it was an underclassman who just had the pulse and respect of the other players. So we used whatever we could to bring us closer as a team and as a family.

Then there were times you had to use the bad example to teach. We've had times when we had to sit some players because of their conduct. We try to talk to them and instill in them the importance of being good role models. A lot of them never had good role models and they pick up what they see around them. We tried to present a good model for them to follow and erase the negative models from them.

We have a lot of young men who aren't used to being told what to do or being disciplined. Many of them have too much freedom it seems to me. I had problems with that from time. Sometimes you have to be firm. Other times you have to be delicate. Some you have to show tough love. Others you have to coddle a little bit. Anybody who thinks they can deal with every personality the same way is kidding themselves. It take some time. Sometimes I forgot. Some kids responded well after hollering at them after practice. And other ones it just destroyed everything you were doing to build them up. Then you have to take a step back and talk about it a little bit.

It goes back to that family atmosphere. You adjust to make it work. You congratulate. You discipline. You prepare them for life. You do it all in love. The more you communicate to them what you are doing and why you are doing it, the more they will understand. Once they get it instilled in them, it will be like second nature. It's the same thing I tell them about character. I tell them when you consistently do what you are supposed to, you'll do it without even noticing that you're doing it. When they were in the gym running drills, I couldn't watch everybody all the time. But if you go out there and run every drill as if someone is watching, that effort will translate every time. You'll do it when you're not told to.

As a team, that becomes contagious. And we all know that success breeds success. If you instill the right principles in early and you consistently work them together, you have no choice but to succeed. That's what it's all about.

James Kahn coached at the Peabody High School in Pittsburgh, Pennsylvania, for 18 years before retiring in 2009. The school closed its doors just a couple years later. For 12 years prior to coaching at Peabody, he coached at Gladstone Middle School.

THE IMPORTANCE OF SYSTEM
SHANE DREILING

Teamwork is the idea of people serving each other for the higher call. On the court, it's making each other better so we can achieve wins. But as a basketball program, teamwork is helping each throughout. For life, it's teaching them how to work with others to be successful or to get something accomplished.

I played sports and had good role models. I had coaches that helped me out and that I've been able to learn from. Most of the coaches that I look up to and that I followed or leaned on throughout the years for advice, go over and beyond what's read about in the newspaper or what's seen on the floor, even though they are highly successful on the floor. I think most coaches, if you ask them, at least I hope, would want a program that is excelling in a variety of areas. I always thought it was relatively easy to have a team that all they do is win or have a team that all they do is excel in the classroom or have a team that all they do is be great at going into the community and helping others that way. What's tough is being able to develop a program that's doing all three and doing all three consistently. From playing it and seeing the coaches up close, helped a lot.

I got a chance to visit with Coach Dean Smith at the University of North Carolina. That really defined what I think a successful basketball program should be. None of the things I saw were revolutionary. But for a young coach or a young man wanting to go into coaching, it's impressive. For example, seeing the idea of freshmen serving the upperclassmen, regardless of what type of skill level or reputation they came in with, taught them the importance of service and humility. It taught them the importance of the system.

The upperclassmen didn't abuse the system or belittle the freshmen either. It was a part of the program that worked for Coach Smith.

The way he did interviews... upperclassmen did interviews. Michael Jordan wasn't interviewed until his junior year. The way he paired players during travel... seniors and freshmen roomed together. They were just little things that built unity and allowed players to help other players develop. He always made it about the team and not the individual.

John Wooden had a good quote that said, a good athlete should have character and not be a character. I always try to handle myself in a classy way. Like most people, I fall short sometimes. But I want people to see our program and say, they are classy. Win or lose, they are going to play the game hard, they're going to respect the game, and respect the program. That's something that is not taught enough. It was my rule that if a kid got a technical, he was done for the game. It probably costs me some games. But to me the idea I'm trying to get across is nothing good is accomplished through anger. When you are a grown man working, anger is not going to help you on your job. It's not going to help you as a husband or a father.

Character has to be taught at home. I'm trying to build on what the parents have done. It's important to me that my programs have a certain image. Even if they are not winning games, the kids are still graduating and the program is still respected. They have to learn through winning and losing and still carry themselves the same.

I am as competitive as anybody and I love to win. Thankfully I've come out on the winning side more than I have on the losing side. But you gotta be careful of what lessons you're trying to get across. There are things I'm not going to do to get a win. I'm not going to break down a kid. I'm not going to cheat. I'm not going to do anything to violate the conduct or the reputation of the program. That's a lesson in and of itself on character and success. What you are trying to accomplish is more than the score. I don't know how much they'll get immediately. I just hope that in the long run they get it. And most of them do.

Shane Dreiling has coached on the professional, college and high school level for over 15 years. He has coached at Newman University and Friends University in addition to the Independent School, Wichita State University, and Goddard High School. He is also author of more than 10 books on basketball and director of TeamArete, an organization that promotes basketball. He currently coaches girls' basketball at Word of Life High School.

86,400 SECONDS
LARRY MCKENZIE

I've been using this creed since I've been coaching. I use it wherever I go. We call it the Polar Creed. This is how it goes:

"This is the beginning of new day. God has given me this day to use as I will. I can waste it or use it for good. For what I do today is important. I'm exchanging a day of my life for it. I must decide whether or not it is good or bad, gain or lost, success or failure, in order to never regret the price that I paid for it."

We live by it.

I really want my guys to know that every day is special, especially in the environment that they live in. There are kids who were yesterday that are not here today so don't take the day for granted. It is a gift.

Ultimately, what I really try to remind my kids about that creed is that it's about self-empowerment. Don't ever give anyone, including myself, the coach, that much power. I don't decide who starts. You decide who starts. But every day, life is about choices, chances and consequences. If you don't come in, you don't work hard, you don't make the right choices, and you take a chance and leave it up to me, you may or may not play. So you must decide every day, good or bad, gain or loss, success or failure.

While you're here at practice, your classmates go home. They go to work. They get to play with their Xboxes. They get to play with their Playstations. But you are here working. Every time those weights go up, every time I want you to think about that 6 minute mile we run, you are reminded that you have paid a price and you want to get something out of it.

I listened to the Super Bowl interview with Russell Wilson. I think it was his father that always asked him, 'Why not you?' And I am saying to my kids in that creed, 'Why not you?' Somebody's going to win the game. Why not you? Somebody's going to win the championship. Why not you? That's what that creed is about. It's a reminder that you have to work hard but more importantly don't give anybody else the control. You control the outcome.

We use it constantly. In the classroom, don't tell me that you can't do it. It's about choices. Don't let teachers have that much control over your goals and your destiny. Do what you have to do. Classroom, family, community... It all comes back to that creed.

John Wooden puts it this way. He says that every morning at the stroke of midnight, the good Lord above gives all of us 86,400 seconds and then we have a choice because it comes with conditions. The condition is what you don't use, you lose. Therefore, are you taking advantage of your 86,400 seconds? Nobody gets 86,300. Nobody gets 86,250. Nobody gets 86,500. It is total equality. Every day at the stroke of midnight we get 86,400 seconds but whatever you don't spend, whatever you don't take advantage of by 11:59 p.m., you lose. So I remind our kids about choices and how you use your time.

I use it in terms of setting goals. How do we get from a 'C' to a 'B' – from a 'B' to an 'A'? You play a significant role in that. And the creed says, This is the beginning of new day. God has given ME – not Coach McKenzie, not your mother, not your uncle – He has given YOU, specifically, this day to use as you will. It's your choice. You can waste it or use it for good.

You don't get a do over. This day has never been and it never will be again. Whatever you don't accomplish this day, you just didn't do it. So every day is important. So you should be able to lay your head on the pillow every night, feeling good. That doesn't mean you are going to get everything done. But the things that you intended to do, the high priorities, you were able to make the right choices.

So I have to decide every morning when I walk out that door, good or bad, gain or lost, success or failure. And those are the things that I try to practice.

Larry McKenzie is the head boys' basketball coach at Minneapolis North High School. He is the only high school coach in Minnesota high school basketball history to win four straight Minnesota State Championships. He is also author of the book, Basketball, Much More than Just a Game.

IT'S FOR THE BIG PICTURE
MICHAEL COOPER

I've had some very good coaches throughout my career. But I think it became more noticeable that I was going to get into coaching after playing for Coach Pat Riley, who was very detailed about his coaching whether it was scouting teams or scouting individuals. At the time, he was doing a little of both. The things he used to set up with scouting tape or things we'd go over in practice made my transition easy because I tried to do a lot of the things that I was taught as a player.

Now passing that on with the men at certain points of my career and now with the women, it's just trying to give my philosophy and the things that I learned and how I've implemented things as a defensive player for the team concept and watching that materialize in practice and then in the game. That's the joy of it for me.

My line is drawn once the game starts. I can't cross that line and go onto the court. So I have to have them prepared mentally and physically to play the game. I think that's when they will see the hard work. When you push them in practice and you make them work hard sometimes they'll say, 'Why are we doing all this running?' It's not for the moment in the beginning. It's for the big picture in the end. We're going to be running when other teams are tired. Practice makes perfect. All of that goes into the preparation for the game.

I think the ultimate thing that we as players and coaches judge success is wins and losses. But for me success is putting your best foot forward and being prepared as I can to play that particular individual, or opponent, for that night. And if we come up short, I know that I gave everything that I had. And for that one particular evening, they were the better team. But if I keep working, eventually, in the long run, I'm going to come out on the winning end at one point in time. So success for me? Yeah, winning that game but if you come up against an opponent that's just as prepared and maybe is a little bit better at home or away, just putting up a good solid effort, knowing that we did everything possible that the officials let us do, and that the ball was able to go into the basket, if we come up one point losers, that to me can still be a successful night. You try to build on those particular nights when you come up short so that in the end, that one year, that one big game, you come up a winner. Success for me is just the preparation and dedication that you put in to that particular performance that night.

Obviously when you tell people you've won this many championships or that many championships, that alone sets the precedent for you knowing what it takes for you to win a championship. So at any level, men or women, they understand that this guy been there and done that. So now if he knows how to do it, let's listen to him, dedicate what we have as an individual and as a team, to follow his rules and follow the steps that he's trying to show us to get there. It's going to take a little bit of you getting it done. It's different from me being out there and you being out there. Winning championships is a pedigree that kind of comes with the territory. Anybody you've been around that you want to be successful in whatever endeavor you want to do in life, you're going to listen to whatever that person did to get it done and then put forth that effort.

For me, I never won a championship until I got to the pros. I had been there many times but never won. Being in the pros is a heightened feeling because all the work that you put into all the work that you do – the practices, the sweat and tears, a lot of the wins and a lot of the losses – you get out there and stopping one of the greatest players who ever played the game in Larry Bird, or Dr. J, or Michael Jordan. That's a good feeling because it's something that you actually had a hand in doing. But when you coach a group of players, whether it be men or women, with your philosophy that you have inside that you feel is the best particular route for this team, that's a little bit more of a greater feeling because you can't get out there and shoot a free throw. You can't stop anyone. It all has to be done with your philosophy and your knowledge. Both of those are great and the first time winning with the Lakers was great. But winning as a coach is a little bit more special.

Michael Cooper is head coach of the WNBA's Atlanta Dream. He won back-to-back championships as coach of the Los Angeles Sparks in 2001 and 2002. In 2006, he won the NBA D-League championship with the Albuquerque Thunderbirds. He won five championships playing with the Los Angeles Lakers.

WE ALL GROW
BOB HUGGINS

If you're getting better day to day, then you're doing something right.

When I recruit players and I talk to their parents about them coming to play for me, I don't make a bunch of promises that I can't keep. But what I do promise them is that I'm going to give 100 percent to provide the tools they need to be successful. We try to create an environment where they can be successful.

I believe they realize the tremendous opportunity in front of them to use basketball to get an education and prepare them for success in life, whether they make it to the NBA or find success somewhere else.

Am I hard on my guys? Sometimes. Do I push my guys? Absolutely. Do I love my guys? I sure do. Nobody believes in my players more than me. Ask them. They will tell you that. Not all of them get it at first. But that's a part of growing up. We all grow. The things we try to implement as part of our program is designed to help these young men grow and be successful. I never say, 'I told you so,' when they come back and say, 'Coach, you were right.' That's why I coach because I love basketball. I have a passion for basketball. But I love the fact that I can help these young men grow.

We don't always do everything right. I know I haven't done everything right in my life. I let them know that we have to learn from our mistakes because that's part of the growing process. We try to build relationships with the players so they know they can come to us when they have problems, whether it's about basketball or not. That's the key. You have to communicate and build relationships.

Bob Huggins is head men's coach at West Virginia University, where he's been since 2007. He began his coaching career as an assistant coach at WVU after his playing career ended there in 1977. He also coached at Kansas State, Cincinnati, Akron, Central Florida, Walsh, and Ohio State. His teams have made the postseason in 25 of 28 seasons, including two Final Fours.

'FAMILY' IS NO CLICHÉ HERE
ALAN HUSS

I think the one thing that each year teaches me is that I need to take a step back because the kids are the ones who have to want it and have to get it. Early in my career I was so hungry for success and so hungry to climb the coaching ladder, pile up victories and maybe move on to the next job. Now that I'm at a place that I love so much, I've learned to take a step back and let my assistants take ownership in this thing, let my players take ownership in this thing. I think since we've done that the last couple years, we've taken it to the next level because I think our players feel they are a part of the leadership of this deal and my assistant coaches definitely feel like they have more ownership in it. I think that all fed into the culture that we have here.

There are so many different ways you can define success. I think by nature, high school basketball, especially at the highest level, is developmental in nature. For us, a successful kid is a kid who is able to go into a college basketball program that they choose and they are prepared to be a valuable member of their team, a valuable member of their school community, able to be successful from the start in the classroom and also obviously on the basketball court and the community as a whole.

I think so many college athletes, and even high school students, take that part for granted. That's something we take a lot of pride in encouraging our kids to get out and be a part of something other than basketball. I think a truly successful kid will understand the value of each of those areas and be prepared to take advantage of the things that not only our school has to offer but the university as well.

I think I'm spoiled. Our school is such a tight-knit school and does such a phenomenal job of teaching so many of those lessons that makes it easy on me. When kids buy into La Lumiere School they've learn so many of those lessons outside of the classroom and outside of basketball. Our part as basketball coaches is just encouraging them to seek those opportunities out and take advantage of them. We're blessed. We have great kids. They get a little closer sooner. We've had great kids that came from great families. Our families have done a great job of helping kids realize the value of what they're experiencing. As long as they come in with an open heart and an open mind, they seem to really buy in pretty quickly.

It is a cliché… the basketball family deal. But when you get into a boarding situation like ours, it really holds true. We really are their family away from their primary family because for nine months of the year, they live here. For us, cultivating a family atmosphere is a vital part of our success. I think between the people in our program, my assistant coaches, and some of the people outside of the program, the dorm parents, teachers… it's a little different. It truly is a family. It's a group of guys who really care about each other and wants to see each other successful on and off the floor.

I think this is our best chemistry group that we've ever had. I think we've maximized our abilities. I like the fact that they like to hang out with each other outside of basketball and they love to share the basketball on the floor. As a coach, that's what it's about. It's not about just straight up winning games. It's the way you win. As I get older, the way you win is as important. The way that we've won this year has been fun to watch because our guys have won the right way. They've won with class and a level of unselfishness that I haven't seen in 10 years. We don't have a guy that cares about scoring baskets on our team. We have guys that care about winning and cares about each other.

Alan Huss is head boys basketball coach at La Lumiere High School in La Porte, Ind. He recently finished his fourth year at La Lumiere, where is also assistant director of admissions, and previously coached at Culver Military Academy. Huss played collegiately at Creighton University.

RELATIONSHIPS, LEARNING AND SUCCESS
ANNE DONOVAN

I wasn't one who came up thinking I wanted to be a coach. I was playing pro ball. I played six years overseas, before the WNBA, obviously. I had some health issues that kind of abruptly finished my career. Not sure what I wanted to do, the coach at my alma mater, Old Dominion, roped me into being a volunteer coach. It's kind of how it started. I quickly learned that it was extremely difficult and challenging and nothing that I thought as a player. You have no real understanding of what coaches do but it's so rewarding and fulfilling and it's almost addicting right from the start.

As young players we just assume you go out there and practice on the things like shooting or defense. You have no idea about the statistical analysis and the in-depth preparations that goes behind a simple a practice plan. I had no idea of that until I got started.

Because I had played for so long, I entered coaching as… a player's coach is pretty cliché but I would definitely say that. The first couple years there were players who weren't seeing eye-to-eye with the head coach. So just figuring out how to push their buttons to find more success as a player, for them to see life a little differently, to see a different perspective as a person… those are the things that I found rewarding.

I was captain on a lot of teams that I played for – Olympic teams, college teams, and national teams. I was very shy… I'm not your typical outgoing coach. I guess there was some leadership tendencies that I think were innately developed when you come from a family of eight kids and I was the youngest of eight kids. You're learning leadership and followship at a very young age. I think they parlayed into the basketball realm for me.

When I was 5, my father passed away so it was a single mother with eight kids. I had seven brothers and sisters. Everybody was tall. Everybody played basketball. Six of us went to college on scholarship which was obviously important for us. I learned the game in the back yard with my brothers and sisters. As a kid, in a family, and then as a player for the different teams I played for, I kind of inadvertently, unconsciously, learned what I would do and what I wouldn't do, what worked for me and what didn't work for me. Although I didn't aspire to be a coach, I had a great case study in the home and because I played for so many coaches throughout college and beyond.

Everybody has a voice. We encourage the players to have a voice, and question any concerns or share different perspectives. I don't like being the only voice in the room. I believe that leadership has to come from different voices. It is a team and everybody needs to have a voice. That needs to be encouraged.

In the pro game, teamwork is the most important component. It's something that needs to stay in the game. I love it. It's people from different backgrounds buying into the same goals and having the same aspirations, channeling all of their energy and focus into one direction. I don't know that I give them examples, in terms of big picture. But every film breakdown, every scouting report, everything we do, that I've done successfully, has been about team. It's how the *team* is going to attack another team or how *we're* going to accomplish our goals. I can't say I do it right all the time but I continue to do it. Even this last season, I'm learning how to do better.

With every situation you have things to take in and adjustments to make and that's why I love basketball. When I go back to the Connecticut Sun, it's going to be a different complexion of players, different sets of issues, and challenges, and strengths. I think that's why I love the game so much. You figure out how the common denominator of team is going to overcome all.

There is nothing I've accomplished as a player that is as rewarding as being a coach and watching someone else succeed. God medals as a player pale in comparison to the gold medal that we won in 2008 when I coached that Olympic team. There is nothing like that feeling of watching others succeed. In a lot of cases that means players are still calling me, they're asking for advice, I'm watching them be successful coaches or incredible mothers. It comes in different ways. But that's what it's about. I'm still involved with basketball because it's about relationships. That's what keeps me going. I love that aspect of our game.

Anne Donovan is the head coach of the WNBA's Connecticut Sun. She has also coached the Seton Hall University, Indiana Fever, Detroit Shock, Charlotte Sting, and Seattle Storm, where she won a championship. In 2008, she coached the USA women's Olympic gold medal team. She won two additional gold medals as a player and a national championship at Old Dominion. She was inducted into the Naismith Basketball Hall of Fame in 1995.

ALL ABOUT THE ABC'S
PATRICK WALTON

Each coach normally has a philosophy. Our philosophy over at Voyager Academy is called the ABCs, which are academics, basketball, character, and support. It's in no particular order but these are the things that we stress in our program. That pretty much lays down the foundation of what we're trying to do.

Being a student-athlete, academics come first, if you want to play a sport at all. So we definitely make sure they get what they need to get the work done in the classroom. We always stress academics. We always stress the importance of going to college. We expect all of our kids to graduate. But we're expected them to graduate college.

Basketball, of course, takes a lot. You have to work hard on your craft every day, especially for those who are serious about it. It's the little things that we do such as offseason, pre-season, and postseason. We only have two months that we take off during the year dead period.

Character is real big because that involves the life skills that we keep talking about with each one of our student athletes…being accountable, knowing what it's like to be a leader. Learning little things like sacrifice, dedication and respect that it's going to take in order for you to accomplish anything good. So we definitely set our standards high. Things like sportsmanship is preached every day and having a positive attitude to having a positive outlook on life. The glass is half full.

Finally we have support. You can't accomplish anything great without having someone around to share it with, having people to back you up, and supporting you. So everything that we've been able to accomplish with our basketball program is because the fans, the families, the parents, teachers, coaching staff, cheerleaders… everybody involved. It's important to have that support around you because it makes what you are trying to do a little bit easier.

I got into coaching around 2004 at East Chapel Hill High School. I volunteered there for a year then I was fortunate enough to get a head JV job the next year and I was there until 2010. I always knew that I wanted to run my own basketball program. But it was pretty much learning under Coach Hartsfield who's a great coach, who won the state championship in his first year and has been there ever since the school opened in '96. I finally got the opportunity by word of mouth and got the opportunity to coach at Voyager Academy in 2010.

Basically we started from the ground up with just a group of freshmen. We started our first year and it was a tough process. People really didn't want to try out for a program when they knew it was new and you were going to take a lot of bumps in the road. So we started off with a record of 2-17. The next year we had freshmen and sophomores. We played a varsity schedule against juniors and seniors in the state. We finished 8-16, last in our conference and no invite to the state tournament. And then last year, now that we had a junior class, we ended up finishing second in our conference and we won the conference tournament championship. We were able to be ranked as high as 25th in the state and we had a solid season. This past year, we were able to finish 20-10, we got a #4 seed for the state playoffs, we won our regular season and conference tournaments, and finished as high as 15th in the state. So it's definitely been a process.

I call it a VAB Process, something I started on Twitter. Everything that you do takes a process. The VAB stands for Voyager

Academy Basketball Process. It's just a constant reminder to the kids and everybody that when you want to get somewhere and you want to do something, it takes that hard work, sacrifice, and dedication. So being at Voyager, this makes the fourth year I've been coaching there, we've done three years of varsity basketball.

The things that I've been able to get out of it are the impact that I've been able to make on young men and of course the impact they made on me. Normally most people think that as coaches we get to have a strong influence on kids that we coach. Well, it goes the other way as well. They're able to have influences on us as well. It's the kids, themselves, that make us better coaches, better people. Every time I have a team, I pretty much adopt however many players I have. So if I have 12 kids that year, that's how many I adopted as my own. Their problems are my problems. Their successes are my successes. So it definitely has a big impact. It makes you appreciate all the little things that sports teach us. You can be at a high one second and a low the next second. It really keeps you about family, how to be together and how to stick together. The impact that they have on you and you have on them, is priceless.

Patrick Walton is head boys basketball coach at Voyager Academy in Durham, North Carolina. He led the school to its first conference championship and first appearance in the state playoffs. Walton is also founder and director of Sharp Shot Basketball, LLC, an organization that teaches the fundamentals of the game of basketball.

OUT OF YOURSELF AND INTO THE TEAM
SARA LEE

Success to me is getting a group of young women on the same page to accomplish the same goal and striving every day to do that. It's not about just being better basketball players but being better people. That would be success for me. We always want to win but that is not our main focus. If we can take care of the qualities that lead to success, we can be successful.

I think we've gotten into this profession because we like to have an impact on young people's lives. So for me to be successful at what I do I have to contribute to the development of the student athlete over the course of their four years at Denison and hopefully they'll bring some of those lessons from our coaching and use them in other parts of their lives to be successful.

There have been lots of moments where we've been able to make that connection. I think that with adversity and them coming to me, there is a moment of sadness or adversity somewhere in their lives, that's when they turn to the people they care about or that they want to share it with. I think that shows us that we're having an impact on their lives. After they graduate and they come back or they call you and want to have coffee with you, I think that shows that their time at Denison was important to them and their time spent with you was important to them. You were an important person in their lives.

Two years ago we were wanting one of my former players to come back and be my assistant coach. She came back and just her articulating the impact that I had on her while she was here impacted her wanting to get into coaching. She wanted that experience.

When I started coaching I wasn't exactly sure what that experience would be like but as you age it develops and grows. I think the impact is more important to you and the impact that they have on you is more important as you age. I think at first you're a young coach and you take it for granted. You're into winning games and less of the process. As you age, you're into the process much more than the results.

When you're taking yourself a little too seriously in other aspects of your life and you walk down the gym and you have 20 smiling women acting goofy and funny, it makes you enjoy the experience and makes you see what's important. They have certainly been there for me when I needed an outlet. Coaching can be an outlet as well… spending time with young, vibrant people. Being together is what it's about.

We have some team slogans and our big one is, 'Out of yourself and into the team.' It's not just about signing up to be on a team but about making a commitment to be part of a team. It's not about you anymore. It's about the team and the team comes first. I think that's a tough thing for some 18- to- 22-year-olds to get but by the time they go through the process they understand that in life it's not just about them. They have to look out for others and others' feelings. We really stick that message out there. We use that throughout, even with hard work. If you're not working hard, it impacts other people. You might not want to work hard but you have to think about those people that you care about and the people that you really enjoy and like and you want to do it for them if you can't do it for yourself. So we use that message for everything that we do.

It's such a great feeling when you see a team like each other and really enjoy each other. You don't always have that. I've coached for 25 years now and had a little less than 45 teams that I've coached and they don't always like each other. This year, they like each other.

And because of that we've been successful. Everybody's on the same page. Everybody has received the same message. They enjoy each other and that's what it's all about. Their success has been better, in terms of win-losses, because they like each other and they support each other and it's not just for themselves.

Sara Lee is the head women's basketball coach at Denison University in Granville, Ohio. She just completed her 25th season as head coach and also serves as associate athlete director at the university. Lee is the all-time victories leader at the school in women's basketball and volleyball, which she coached for 18 years.

OUTWORK THE NEXT PERSON
TERRY PORTER

I've had the pleasure of playing for some amazing coaches over the years. Many of them told me they thought I would make a good coach someday. At the time I never thought much about it because my passion was playing. I wasn't one of the guys that thought I could play forever but I was just focused on what I was doing.

But later on in my career I gave it a little more thought because I love the game. I knew I wanted to do something around the game. I was a student of the game and I've always been a competitor so people said it would be a natural fit.

I was excited to get an opportunity to share my interpretation on the game, to share my work ethic with young players, teach the fundamentals, teaching defense, and continue to produce quality basketball. Of course I want to win, too, but I want to teach the game. I want to help players develop and get the most out of their potential.

But it'll take hard work. That's how I was raised. You had to work for everything you got. I learned my work ethic at a young age. You might not be the biggest, the fastest, or the strongest player on the court but if you outwork the next person, you can get an advantage. I learned that from the best of them.

Some things just make sense. The things that make sense and that work, you keep doing them. If they don't make sense and they don't work, then don't do them anymore.

Terry Porter is an assistant coach with the Minnesota Timberwolves. After a 17-year playing career in the NBA, he joined the Sacramento Kings as an assistant coach in 2002. The following year, the Milwaukee Bucks hired him as head coach. Porter also coached in Detroit and Phoenix.

MIND CANDY AND COMMUNICATION
DON SHOWALTER

The fulfilling part of coaching any sport, basketball for me, is the relationships you have with players and coaches and parents. You development these relationships with the amount of time you spend with these players over the course of the year and during the offseason. These relationships can be very strong and you have a great connection with the players. Obviously some players might buy in more to what you want done than others but at the same time part of our jobs as coaches is to make every player realize his.

I've been very fortunate to coach some players at the USA Basketball level such as Jabari Parker. If they are that talented, certainly they want to win. They're going to buy into what it takes to win at that level. Then we have other players that are on the high school team that might be my sixth, seventh, or eighth player on the team who also is in the same situation who also wants to be a better player but just isn't that talented yet. But the coaching comes in when, hopefully, you have the player realize the level he can get to and make a plan for him to get to that level.

Our main job coaching at the USA Basketball level is to take away the individual characteristics a little bit from each player and blend those characteristics and level of competition to their teammates. They're all the best players on their teams and you're trying to bring them together to make a team. I've often said at times they're so good they don't have to compete on every possession on our USA team. But as a coach you want them to understand that this is something that you want them to work on and be aware of and compete every possession regardless of how good they are. You try to get them to play for what's on the front of their jerseys as opposed to the individual. We've been very fortunate to have that. The players understand that if they do that they're going to have great success. Again, they're competitive and they want to win so at the highest level for our youth 17 to 16 kids they buy into the fact that we're here to make our teammates better and get a gold medal.

Every day before practice, we have a team meeting and part of that team meeting we have what we call mind candy where we go over a saying or two or a phrase or two that might hit home that day. Then we expand on that and have the players comment on that piece of mind candy. For instance, one thing might be, 'There's a big difference between competing and just playing the game.' Now how does that reflect on the team, how does that reflect on us and how does that reflect on you? We try to get good communication with the players and get them to understand that we're all working to try to get them to be the best that they can become. Another phrase is, 'Hard work beats talent when talent doesn't work hard.' Now how does that reflect on us? We go through that each day with a different set of mind candy. I think that's really been helpful for us.

At the end of practice, we always have what we call a communications circle, where the players get in a circle, hold hands and we have them turn to a player on either side of them and express what they like about his game. They go around the circle communicate that to each other. The next day it might be go around the circle and tell the next player what you felt about today's practice, what can be improved for tomorrow. Good communications can let the players bond in a way that they feel comfortable.

We bring in 30 players for our tryout and only 12 go on the trip so not everybody will make it. But after the tryouts, which last about 4-5 days, they have a greater understanding of what it means to play for a team like USA Basketball and how they have to blend in and give up some of their individual performances for the betterment of the team.

Don Showalter is head boys basketball coach at Iowa City High School. He has been coaching high school basketball for 40 years. In addition, he coaches the USA Basketball Developmental National Team, winning several gold medals.

CARRYING THE TRADITION
DIEGO JONES

It was an honor coming back and being able to coach at my alma mater. Being a student-athlete at the school, you don't really know all of the stuff that goes on behind the scenes other than the rich tradition that came before us. Being a coach and an administrator, it's definitely different. There are a lot more things that go on but you still have to fill that role of trying to carrying out the history.

When I first started coaching back in 2000, I was the head JV coach at the time and a varsity assistant. Those kids back then didn't have all of the negative distractions with the social media and websites, plus all of the other outside distractions. I know we had some distractions but there seems like there are even more now. AAU is a bigger influence on the kids in our area. So you are battling with the AAU coaches, the parents, the agents – not professional agents but street agents. It's a complicated situation. I wouldn't necessarily say it was pressure for me but I knew that I had a job to do to uphold the major tradition of the school.

The biggest challenge has been the kids not really focusing on the education. Our school is not a zone school where just anybody can get into the school easily. You have to have a 3.0 grade point average along with a certain test score. Kids have been turned away because they couldn't make it. I'm talking about high quality, high character kids that just didn't have the scores. So sometimes it's been a challenge. From a basketball standpoint, that has kind of hurt the tradition of the school and that's why you see so many kids around the city going to private schools because they are governed under a different administration.

It was my passion and my experience with the game of

basketball that made me want to come back and give back to the kids in our area. It wasn't my concentration to come back to Dunbar High School but I always felt as though I wanted to teach. I wanted to give back. I just love working with the kids. I know they are our future and I know they need guidance. A lot of the kids don't have positive father figures or role models that they can really relate to or get something positive from. That's why a lot of them fall victim to the street.

I'm constantly preaching life situations to the kids through practice, after practice, through games, after games. I basically use whatever experiences I see that I share with them. I also share stories with them about my life. I tell them I grew up in Baltimore City just like you. Not having my father in my life as a youngster, I thrived off playing sports. I knew sports were going to be my outlet. I looked at successful people and stated that I wanted to be like them. Those things and those people helped push me. So I tell them they need to do the same thing. Find your goal first and at the same time, look at the people around you who are positive and put some of these people in your circle instead of these negative people. Successful people are the ones you want to emulate. You don't want to deal with the negative people because all they do is bring you down.

I try to lead them into doing positive things that will help them become successful. Every day I tell them, continue to gain success and continue to move forward.

Diego Jones is head boys basketball coach at Dunbar High School in Baltimore, Md., where helped lead the school to a national championship as a player in 1992. As a coach, he led the school to four straight state championships from 2010-2013.

SOMETHING'S GOING TO HAPPEN
RYAN HUMPHREY

I've been blessed to be around the game of basketball at a high level for at least 20 years. I was a McDonald's All American so I played at a high level, played in the NBA and all over the world. I felt like coaching would an easy transition because I know the game from a player's perspective and I know how the game of basketball can take you all around the world. I played under Hubie Brown. I played under Doc Rivers. I played under the best minds internationally as well so I've been able to pick up some things along the way.

I know that not everyone will be able to play in the NBA but you can still make a living and play professionally overseas. Everyone might not be able to play overseas but you can still be a productive man just by playing the game of basketball and getting a good education.

A lot of the guys that I've been around don't have male figures. I was blessed to have male figures in my life in my dad and my older brother. But a lot come from single-parent homes and a lot of coaches do take on that father figure role. A lot of guys lean on the coaches to give them that tough love that they can't get at home.

I'm from Tulsa and I've always been able to work out at Tulsa University in the offseason when I was playing. I was working out there for about 8 or 9 years. When Coach Manning transitioned there and took over the program, I kind of kept the rapport. Thanked him for allowing me to work out there while I was playing and when I transitioned and said this is it, I went and I sat down with him. I was coming to practice and one of the guys said, 'Why don't you take on a volunteer assistant role? This will allow you to do more.' So I thought it was the perfect place to do it under Coach Danny Manning's umbrella. So I'm learning everything that he brought from Kansas and what he learned from Larry Brown and his NBA philosophy. So I am gleaning everything I can from him.

Basketball is an extended family. What happens is you end up spending more time with the guys just as much as you do with your natural family. So it is a close-knit family. You see guys up and down. You see something happen off the floor and they bring it on the floor too. So you learn guys' moods. You learn to see what makes guys tick. You see the growth process between the guys just like you see with your kids.

Basketball translates to life in that you won't always get your way. But if you work at it and be persistent, good things will happen. It's just like in life, sometimes you get bad bounces but if you keep working and be persistent, eventually something's going to happen.

I've been blessed to have a lot of coaches that I keep in contact with. One thing one coach taught me was that if you take care of your game, you game will take care of you. Which means that if you put the quality time in, you really take care of your game, basketball will be able to take you to places you never thought you would see. I've been blessed to play in 9-10 different countries. If I hadn't taken care of my game I wouldn't have been able to see some of these things like the Eiffel Tower.

But you have to work at it. It's easy to come in the gym when the team is in there but it's what you do behind the scenes when you are by yourself. It's easy to be a part of a family when things are good. But when things hit the wall, or you're in a slump, your coming in the gym when no one is in there, putting up thousands of shots… is what makes the difference.

Ryan Humphrey is a volunteer assistant coach on head coach Danny Manning's staff at Tulsa. A former first round draft pick of the Utah Jazz and then traded to the Orlando Magic on draft night in 2002, Humphrey played professionally, including overseas until 2013. This is his first season as a coach.

SPORTS TEACH LIFE LESSONS
DWAYNE CHERRY

I've always been a school teacher since I graduated college and my heart has always been in sports. I had a group of kids who didn't have anywhere to play. With AAU being so expensive, my wife and I took it on ourselves to start our own about 7-8 years ago. Once we got that established, I started working with kids even more.

That led to my coaching at middle school and then high school, first at Independent High School, which brought me to Charlotte Country Day.

These were good kids who just didn't have a chance to play because maybe they were from single parent homes, or they didn't have transportation to practices and tournaments, or financially they couldn't afford to pay the registration fees. And these were talented players and great kids. I felt like it was important to at least give them an opportunity to play AAU ball. For a number of them, it landed them an opportunity to play in college. Had that not had that experience then that college opportunity might not have been there for them.

Because of my experience playing sports, I really have a heart to see kids reach their maximum potential. I feel like I didn't accomplish everything that I could have so when I see talented kids, something just kind of stirs up in me to try to help them reach their maximum potential.

I made sure the time that I spent with them was not just about basketball. We would do things outside of basketball – go to the mall or go by their school to check up on them. I'd even meet with their guidance counselors and their academic advisors to make sure they were taking the right classes, SAT prep classes. I wanted to make sure we dealt with life lessons so that once they made it to college or even after college, they'd be able to take those lessons and used them.

My teaching background actually helps my coaching. You learn so many strategies on how to teach in the classroom, especially with the population I worked with before coming to Charlotte Country Day. I was working in the inner-city, lower income schools. You have so many levels of students in your classroom so you might be teaching one lesson but you have different levels of learners. That carries over onto the basketball court. You are into the habit of making sure everybody understands what I'm saying. I'm really big on everybody doing something all the time. So I don't have 6-7 guys on the sidelines watching because that was instilled in me as a classroom teacher. So I will have one group working on ball handling and another group working on shooting and an assistant coach down the other end going over plays, just so that everybody can be engaged and learning.

There have been a number of experiences where they have taught me as well. Sometimes a kid will bring experiences that you don't have. They have a different perspective or insight that you might not have. I came from a two-parent home so I don't have the experience of a kid from a single-parent home. It makes me adjust and be sensitive to kids in those situations and be able to better understand those situations. And now I'm better able to handle these types of situations in the future because I've had those experiences. And like the kids, I'll have life lessons that I can carry on for the rest of my life.

The one thing I tell everybody is that sports teach life lessons. Even with my two kids starting to play sports. That's the main thing goal I hope they get out of it. Whether they become college or professional athletes, to me, is not really a goal.

Dwayne Cherry is head boys basketball coach at Charlotte Country Day School in Charlotte, NC. He has more than 10 years including AAU, middle school and high school levels.

IT HAS TO START WITH ME
MIKE JONES

This is arguably one of the most famous high schools that there is and our basketball program is a big piece of the notoriety that our school gets. Most of that is because of Coach Morgan Wooten. Both gyms here were named after him. With the banners we have around and the pictures on the wall and recent history with so many of our guys that are in college doing well, there is the constant reminder of the tradition and the standard. We don't need to tell the kids because it's everywhere they look. When we're practicing, Morgan Wooten's name is up on the wall. When we're going to the locker room, there are pictures of Victor Oladipo and Jerian Grant on the wall. When they go home at night and watch college basketball, there are constant reminders of DeMatha with our guys playing.

For a lot of them, that's why they chose to come here. They are chasing that same recognition and notoriety and most importantly the opportunity to play college basketball and get a free education. I would say the consistent message is our school's motto is we are gentlemen and scholars. We want to uphold the highest of standards in terms of our effort in the classroom and then at DeMatha we're used to winning so we want them to be gentleman, winners and champions so they have to give that same effort on the court.

With youth today there is a sense of entitlement that we have to combat and battle. Ultimately, it's so competitive here that entitlement doesn't bode well for you. People don't respond too well to that if we are not successful. You might come in with it and you might expect it to happen because you have DeMatha on your chest or jersey but ultimately, you're opponent doesn't care. If anything, it's more motivation for them to beat you. Our guys learn that relatively quickly.

I can imagine but I can't say I know what it's like to be a teenager in this era. I have no idea. When I went home from school, I went to play basketball, on an outdoor court with my friends. Video games? We had some but they weren't like they are now. You have people making careers out of playing video games. That definitely didn't exist when I was coming up. I couldn't tell you if I had all of these other options in terms of things to do. I would like to think I would have been as committed as I was to being the best basketball player I was but I don't know that for a fact. So I feel for the guys somewhat. What I try to do is give them – not 24-hour access – but full access to being able to get in and get shots up, to get in the weight room to try to get stronger. But with our staff, with any kid who wants to work out, we don't tell them no because you might have a kid trying to be like it was 25 years ago but they're told no once or twice and they lose the desire to do it. We never want to have that with one of our guys.

Obviously as a leader of men, there are times I'm going to have to make decisions or hold them accountable for things. But I respect their parents and they respect me. I don't want the parents to coach and I'm definitely not going to parent them. If mom and dad says you can have an earring, I'm not going to tell you you can't. That's not my job. You just can't have one when you're doing things with our team. I try to play my role and play it as well as I can.

Every family is different. Some guys don't have a father at home. By default they're going to look at me as that male role model and I understand that. I do what I'm asked to do and I don't try to do more than that. We try to keep everything in perspective with defined roles and accountability.

I don't believe in excuses. I don't believe in blaming others for shortcomings or failures. I don't want our kids to that. So if something goes wrong, I want you to look at yourself and figure out what you could've done differently. When the opportunity presents itself again, and hopefully it does, then maybe you can approach it with a better plan. With the game of basketball, with athletics or sports in general, a lot of times you don't play as much as you want to and it's the coach's fault. Or you didn't score as many points as you wanted to and it was because your teammate didn't pass you the ball. This happened in the game because the referee didn't call the foul. It's always somebody else's fault instead of saying, 'Had I shot more free throws in the offseason maybe I'd be shooting a better free-throw percentage,' or 'Maybe if I had worked a little bit harder to get open my teammates would have passed me the ball,' or 'Maybe if I had been in better shape the coach would have played me sooner.' I totally believe in this. After every game, I think, 'What could I have done differently?' It has to start with me, then what could we have done differently.

Mike Jones is the head boys basketball coach at DeMatha High School in Hyattsville, Md. He just completed his 11th season after taking over for Hall of Fame Coach Morgan Wooten. Jones earned his 300th career win earlier this year. He was also named coach of the 2014 USA Junior National Select Team.

THE DEMATHA OF THE MIDWEST
KYLE LINDSTED

I remember my first practice and telling my team that we were going to be the DeMatha of the Midwest. I know that I was a running joke but that's what I believed we were going to be, a powerhouse in the middle of the country. The last two years we finished in the top 10 in the nation. It's taken a while to get there and continuity has been a big thing. But having a philosophy and having guys understand your philosophy, preaching it every day and working at it every day and really believing that you're going to make it, have helped.

We've won some championships, got some titles and awards. But the sweetest accomplishments are when you see lives changed. Young men are better students, better people and better players as a result of coming through our program.

As I was developing as a coach, I read all of Morgan Wooten books. I just knew that they were a top program and his philosophy and his ideals about life and character and what he tried to develop in his players was something that I really wanted to mirror. I wanted us to be a national program and still do things the right way. There's a lot of people who want success and not a lot of people want to do it the right way. But he was a guy that I looked at and said he's doing things that right way. He's got his priorities right.

There is a kid that's a sophomore at OU right now. His name is Buddy Hield. He's projected at 30 to 40 in the draft as a sophomore. I saw Buddy in the Bahamas. I went down for a basketball tournament. He was about 6'1" – 145 pounds. He wasn't the most athletic player. He wasn't by any means the top player in the gym. But I just noticed his character and his charisma and his passion for the game. His service toward his teammates on the court and the humility that he played with drew me to him. He came to Sunrise as a junior and now he is 6'4" and when he left here he was 205 pounds. He really grew as a man. To see a kid in that environment and where he is today athletically and academically and put him in an environment that could basically change his whole life. Now he's looking at the draft. He came from a little guy growing up playing on milk crates with a piece of plywood nailed to a telephone pole. Now he's the leading scorer at Oklahoma University. He's an outstanding young man. He's a yes sir, no sir-type guy. He understands the philosophy he got here at Sunrise and his passion for the game. He has remained humble and grateful for everything he got and everything he is working toward.

Those are the kind of stories as a coach, that when you look back, is greater than any win or loss or any accolade I could actually receive. You see a life that has been touched and changed. His life is changed. His children's lives are going to be changed. That's the best feeling you can have as a coach. That's why we supposed to be in this.

We talk about something morally or spiritually every day with our kids. We make that a point of emphasis. We tell our guys all the time that character is who you are when no one is watching. When you think you are getting away with something, that's who you really are. I think that's something that really hits home with our guys. Basketball is a great way to judge character. You can tell guys that have high character. Are you doing the little things for the team even though they hurt? It's not always pleasant. Sometimes it's work. You take a guy who cut corners in the classroom and he's going to cut corners on the court. Your character is your character. It's real hard to hide it in any aspect of life. Eventually it's going to raise its ugly head if you don't have it together. That's why we want to make sure we are developing better students, better people and better players.

Kyle Lindsted is head boys' basketball coach at Sunrise Christian Academy in Bel Aire, Kan., where he's been coaching since 2000. He has helped the school become one of the top high school programs in the country.

SPORTS IS AN EQUALIZER
BET NAUMOVSKI

Sports is an equalizer. It doesn't matter if you have money or you don't have money, if you're black or you're white. Sports really is an equalizer. So it was a place that I felt that I could go and I felt like I belonged. I felt like everybody else. When we are young and we have doubts about who we are and who what we were going to be, it became a real safe place for me. It didn't hurt that I good at it and I excelled. But as I grew, the meaning of the sport changed for me. It gave me a confidence boost and it helped shape me into the person I am today. I wanted to give that experience to somebody else.

It's a tool to teach life lessons to young people. And hopefully help them develop into leaders and help them develop into who they want to be, whether you want to be a CEO, or have your own business. Hopefully sports will equip you to be successful in whatever you chose to do or be in your life.

Any opportunity that we have to make that correlation, we do. One of the things I want them to understand is that, yes we aim to be successful. And let's face it. If you win it's a whole heck of a lot more fun than losing. But what we want them to understand is that the formula to winning is about more than just winning games. It's about being able to work with different personalities and understand how to set a goal, having the work ethic it takes to achieve a goal, understanding what it means to be a great leader and what it means to be a great follower. We spend more time talking about those things. That's one of the reasons we've had good success. We try to equip them and enable them to solve their own problems. If we haven't developed them into a place where they can solve some of their own problems, in the moment of a game, then we're not doing something right. We're not teaching very effectively. So I take great pride in watching my team play and they're having dialogue on the floor, solving their own problems. That's when I know I've done a good job as a coach.

Winning and success are two different things. We talk more about success than we talk about winning. Just because we're winning doesn't mean we're being successful. It just means I probably did a good job of recruiting. Success is in the goals that we lay down as a team and the work that we're doing to achieve those goals.

We make a point to recruit players with high character. I think we have good talent but we stress high character as well. We lost a game that we shouldn't have lost. That definitely hurt our opportunity for a regional ranking. But the reason why we were in some close games and the reason why we lost that close game to a team that we shouldn't have was that was the week that we were going to teach them some lessons. We sat some of our most talent kids that game. Sometimes when you take something away, that's the shake that they need to let them know that they need to make a change. So we talk a lot about being willing to make changes and not be afraid to make changes. That was our two captains that we sat. So we said you are not doing what we need you to do as leaders off the floor, you're not going to play in these next two games. We had a couple kids who missed study hall and that's the responsibility of the captains to make sure they understand that's important. But we also make sure we take the time to talk to them and they took the initiative to come to us and find out what they needed to do to be better leaders.

So that to me was a success. They're 18, 19, 20, and 21 year olds. They're going to make mistakes. I'm okay with mistakes. I'm not okay with repeated mistakes. But it's what you do after making those mistakes that go a long way with me. Do you learn from them? Do you find solutions? Are you willing to make me a process of finding a solution? If the answer is yes, then you'll do very well in this program. I want them to be able to look back and think to themselves that's an experience that I had that I don't believe I could have had with any other coach or any other program.

Elizabeth 'Bet' Naumovski has coached for 15 years in the United States and Canada. She currently is the head women's basketball coach at Queens College in New York, where she's coached for three years. Other coaching positions include Binghamton University, University of Toronto, University of Guelph and York University.

THE 3 C'S: THE COURT, THE CLASSROOM AND THE COMMUNITY
JILL PRUDDEN

I played my senior year in high school and at Michigan State so I really enjoyed the sport from a lot of different aspects. I liked watching it, I liked playing with it and I wanted to stay connected with it. Early on when I got into coaching it was for the excitement of teaching and building a program for kids who only played 6-on-6 to be able to teach them the 5-on-5 game, the full court, the transition, the baseline to baseline type of game. There were some growing years because you had some kids that excelled on one end of the court or the other. But having to play on both ends of the court was very new.

I loved the teaching of the game. I had some really good coaching staffs so we had some really good camaraderie with the players and the coaching staff. I liked that aspect. I loved the challenges and the strategizing of games. I also liked being able to teach life skills, whether it was the discipline of hard work or getting to practice on time or giving your best and being able to transfer that into life lessons.

I was very blessed to have some very talented players. We spent a lot of time talking about roles and how every piece of the pie was important. We spent a lot of time defining, accepting, and talking about roles that would make us successful. We also did a lot of things off the court to bind the team whether it was team dinners, a party at a kid's house, just different things so that once we're off the court we realize we're all just people. We did some team building where we went to a ropes course so that we could rely on each other. We didn't things with room assignments since we were fortunate enough to do some traveling. We went to the Nike Tournaments,

tournaments for the holidays. We had kids room with different kids just so they could get around other kids and not get cliquish.

Humor is huge with me. Laughing was a big part of it. If you can't laugh at a bunch of situations you'll never have true joy. I've got to be the first one to step back and laugh at myself. I think we had a lot of fun. I can think of different teams and different things.

One of the teams that won the state tournament, I remember one of the things they used to do. They used to sit on the bus and see oldies on the bus and laugh and cut up and just have that fun-loving atmosphere.

We not only set goals in terms of individual and team, but we talked a lot about the three Cs. That was giving your best on the court, which when they were with me was easy because I could see that. But my expectation was that they would also give their best in the community and in the classroom. Those were the three Cs so we spent a lot of time talking about goal setting for academics and being role models in the community and what that looked like to younger players. We talked about going to elementary schools and going to the Girls Club and Boys Club and doing some things. We went to the Ronald McDonald House… just ways to give back. They were leadership roles even if they were born leaders. Just by being on a team it put them in leadership positions. We talk a lot about how those things became life skills.

Jill Prudden was the head girls basketball coach at Oak Ridge High School in Oak Ridge, Tenn., for 31 years. Her accomplishments include more than 900 career wins, three state championships, 27 district championships and 21 regional championships. She is also author of the book, Coaching Girls' Basketball Successfully.

WE WILL ALWAYS BE FAMILY
SCOTTIE RICHARDSON

I have coached for 20 years starting at age 18, winning a state title as a player in North Carolina, an assistant coach in Florida, and a head coach in North Carolina. My father, Dale Richardson, coached for 45 years, winning the 1992 state title in Florida. My younger brother, Reggie, has coached on both coasts, in North Carolina and California.

I am the inventor of the Mad Dog Defense which is used by many former players, assistants, and colleagues who are now coaching on the East Coast. However, my No. 1 goal is mentoring young men both spiritually and athletically. We live by the 4 Bs – Bible, Books, Basketball, and the Babes come last.

The ultimate goal is for my players to come back. Recently I was coaching in a Christmas tournament where I was sitting with a college coach who flew in to scout a few of my players and someone tapped me on the shoulder. As I turned around, I was confronted by a voice that said, 'Coach, how are you doing?' A former player of mine from 11 years ago had been following the progress of our team and wanted to check us out. It was more important to me to have that reunion and conversation with a former player and family member than with a coach at that time.

I rode with a former player, John Repass, to the state championships in North Carolina to catch the action. He is now the head coach at the school I coached him at and won a state title.

When you play for me, we will always be family.

Scottie Richardson is head boys basketball coach and athletic director at Neuse

Christian Academy in Raleigh, NC.

WE NEED TO BE THE BEST LEARNERS
PATRICK RUFENER

I wasn't one of those guys who said as a kid, I wanted to coach. I just didn't want to get away from the game. I didn't know if I wanted to coach but I didn't want to leave basketball. I got started then I thought it was a great opportunity to stay around basketball and have a closer relationship with the kids than a high school teacher would have.

You do get to spend more informal time with the kids than a teacher does and sometimes that allows you to have more impact. I've had parents tell me in the past, can you tell my son to be more serious about his work ethic or he needs to start working harder, any of those core values. If you look at success, the principles are pretty clear, yet not everyone is doing them. They're not necessarily easy but they are simple.

I would have parents thank me and I would say that I only reinforced what you put into place. I didn't do anything special. I was just one more voice that said the same thing. I could say something in the gym and they kid would hear it but they wouldn't hear it from their parent. The natural kid-parent relationship is to resist what mom or dad's telling me to do. But my coach says it too and I know deep down my parents are right but I just don't want to do what my parents ask me to do.

When I coached at Marietta College and the College of Wooster, I worked with a lot of student-athletes that had traditional family where mom and dad were in the picture. But when I went over to Wayne College, I worked with a lot of athletes with split families, or there would be only one parent at the games, and my best player I never saw either one of his parents come to a game. So in that role, I'm coaching but I'm also taking a lead role in helping teach those young men what it's like to be a man.

As much as mom wants to help her son, mom cannot teacher her boy how to be a man. It's bestowed by other men. That was a meaningful role for me.

I teach them that success is not going to be easy so we have to get used to working hard. We want to see results right away but sometimes there's delayed gratification. But if we keep doing the right things, which are working hard, making improvements, over time, we'll be where we want to be. We have to be the best learners. We might not be the best shooters, the best rebounders, or run the best offense. But we need to be the best learners. My teams at Wayne even if we weren't that good at the beginning of the season, we were much better by the end of the season. I credit that to the student-athlete's willingness to listen to that message and say, 'Okay Coach. We're going to learn.'

I want them to take that message long-term, long after I'm done coaching them. What we're really doing is setting them up for the bigger picture. We do it with basketball. Somebody else does it with advising. Somebody else does it as a parent. We're trying to prepare them to make good decisions in the future.

You always want to see results of your efforts. But as a leader, you're not always going to see those results. You know that people are going to get out touch or won't always communicate the things that they learned, but that piece comes a lot longer down the road. When you hear the stories of the great coaches, they're adults toward the end of their lifespan and their coming back thanking their coaches. I love it when I hear from a player saying I really appreciate what you did for me. But it may not happen and that's okay. If I'm going to teach them delayed gratification, I have to be able to live the skill myself.

Patrick Rufener is former head men's basketball coach at University of Akron-Wayne College. He currently serves as athletic director at the school and teaches Sport Ethics, Sport Behavior, Intro to Coaching Basketball and Motivational Aspects of Physical Activity in the Sport Studies and Wellness Education Department.

BE A TRANSFORMATIONAL COACH
LASON PERKINS

I've studied Don Meyer's teachings and spent some time with him in person back in the 90s. I attended his coaching academy two times. On one occasion, I was actually able to stay at his house with him and one of the house guests with me was Billy Donovan, who at the time was coaching at Marshall.

I remember one evening we were all sitting downstairs at a table and he and Coach Meyer were sitting their talking and all if could do was just sit there and listen and take notes. There was some really good information going back and forth there.

Coach Don Meyer has spoken about having a purpose beyond winning in your basketball program. I believe that coaches are in a unique position to reach young men and women and teach them life skills through basketball. Our players will not remember what plays you ran or the defenses used when they are adults. What they will remember are the words you spoke and the actions you took with them. They will always remember the friendships and bonds created with their teammates. I believe it is something special to be called a teammate versus someone I went to school with.

My coaching philosophy has been a mix of everything from different sources, coaches here in the US at the college and professional levels, and there have been some coaches international that have helped shape my philosophy in certain areas. I've been fortunate to be around some really good coaches and then also fortunate to work with some coaches here in North Carolina who have two of the top programs here – Bill Boyette, the head coach at Terry Sanford in Fayetteville, N.C., and Scott McInnis, the head coach at Millbrook High School in Raleigh, N. C. Being around them helped form who I am.

Coaching is relationships. That's really the bottom line. Sometimes as coaches we tend to overlook that. We get so caught up in trying to get your season going that you forget that the kids are doing the work. You really need to build those relationships with those kids. Ultimately, that's what they are going to remember. They're going to remember the relationships, the talks that you had with them, when you were encouraging them.

Joe Ehrmann wrote a book called Inside Out Coaching. He talks about two different types of coaches – transactional coaches and transformational coaches. My goal is to be a transformational coach. I'm really looking to have an impact on their lives. I grew up without a father and the men who had the biggest impact on my life were my coaches.

Coach Lason Perkins is the head boys basketball coach at Chapel Hill High School in Chapel Hill, NC, and has been coaching for 30 years. He is widely respected for his coaching philosophies, and developing and demonstrating offensive and defensive strategies, including the high-low triangle offense.

BUILD CHARACTER
DON RUEDLINGER

It's nothing worse than having kids get beat by 60-70 points. That's not building his character. That's destroying it. So we do a lot of camps to make sure kids are getting better and be able to compete. We really want to build character while we develop and showcase the best that basketball has to offer. We make sure that we teach them some things.

We are a full-service youth organization. We've been doing this a while now. We have programs all over not just in the United States but all over the world, including Mexico, Canada, and Kenya, Africa. This is our 25th anniversary.

We have some of the best players and teams from all over the country and the world play in our championships… Mexico, New Zealand, Canada, Bahamas… And it's still early. So we have a chance to do some special things.

This year during our national basketball championships tournament in Orlando, we're bringing in a keynote speaker to talk to parents and coaches about preparing kids for college. They'll talk about scholarships that are available. This is important to us.

We have to make sure that we provide we provide them with all of the information they need to be successful. We do that on the court with camps and tournaments and we do that off the court with information like this.

Don Ruedlinger is president of Youth Basketball of America, an organization that promotes youth basketball worldwide. It strives to provide opportunities for personal growth and development of youth athletes while also reinforcing positive influences, self-confidence, self-esteem and the ability to excel on and off the court.

ALL IN
PAT SULLIVAN

    I find that success is defined differently by each person because not everyone holds themselves or their program to the same standard. What is deemed as success for one person or program might not meet the standard set by another. For me, success is measured by whether or not our team maximizes its talents and potential in order to achieve our goals. Success is something that is measured in everything we do. To be the best and maximize its potential, a team must see the value in trying to be successful in the smallest details every day in everything they do. Learning how to be successful is a lifelong skill that will benefit the players in life after sports.

    Character development is so important because as coaches we have an obligation to help guide and mentor our players. As a college coach, we become one of the player's biggest role models. While away at college, most of these athletes spend more time with us than they do with their parents. The parents trust us to help prepare their kids for the rest of their lives. Sure basketball is a big part of what we do, but for us at the Division III level, we aren't preparing players to go on to the NBA. Instead, our job is to help prepare them for the rest of their lives. If we can't help them develop into good people of high character then we simply aren't doing our jobs.

    Coaching plays a huge part in developing young people, especially at the college level. We spend so much time together with our players that how we act and carry ourselves is going to influence how our players do. I think playing for a coach who you respect not because he wins a bunch of games, but because he treats you and everyone else on the team fairly and with respect has a powerful influence on the players. I firmly believe that the players are a reflection of their coach. When I see a team play, how the players behave during the game tells me a great deal about how they are being coached and what their coach values. I always think about what do I want others to say about our guys after they get done watching us play? How you act as a coach is going to have a direct impact on how your players act. I think that the values that you model for your players every day are the ones that they are going to carry with them the rest of their lives. Hard work and determination are keys because life is going to throw you a lot of curve balls. How your players see you handling adversity is going to directly influence how they handle it the rest of their lives. When things get hard do you keep your head down and keep grinding away or do you make excuses and put the blame on others? The ability to be all-in when things aren't going your way is a special skill that requires a level of toughness that not everyone has. If you can instill this in your players by the time they graduate and move on to the real world then you are doing your job.

Patrick Sullivan is an assistant coach at Defiance College in Defiance, Ohio He's been on the staff for five years under head coach Kyle Brumett.

USE BASKETBALL AS A VEHICLE
SCOONIE PENN

    I watch a lot of AAU because I have a son now who is 12 and he's been involved with basketball since he was in the fourth grade and he really loves it. So I watch these kids run around but there's not any more teaching. I grew up being taught. There is a difference between teaching and coaching. I feel a lot of people aren't teaching these kids anymore. It's more about what we see on TV. These athletes run around, jump, and shoot threes. There is a reason why not many guys have a mid-range jump shot. A guy shoot but he can't dribble. A guy can dribble but he's not a good outside shooter.

    I remember growing up and watching basketball and guys would have to be able to do it all to be successful. Nowadays they're going off potential. I just feel there is a lost art of really training kids and the game itself is being lost.

    I think it correlates to outside of the game as well. Understand times have changed, but I had a coach that taught sports but was involved in our lives, whether it was at the Boys Clubs of rec centers that kept us out of the streets, that kept us in the gym. But they also spoke to us about the pros and cons of what we do outside of the Boys Club or the rec center or school and how that could impact our lives. I just feel there's not that much anymore. I understand a lot of cities cut budgets and where did they cut budgets? Recreation centers.

    I do a mentoring program every Thursday with some of the worse areas in Columbus and that's what happened. When money goes short, they cut rec centers and things like that that are needed in the community. Then that affects how our kids grow up.

Sports, itself, is a teaching tool. For me, basketball was the ultimate teacher. Lessons that I learned on the court, how to conduct myself, about being disciplined, about working hard, those are the exact same things you need to do and have in life to be successful. So, in one sense, being taught at a young age about becoming a good ballplayer, coaches were also teaching us about being good in life. I think that's what it's about. Being a coach can really help kids by letting them understand that basketball is great. Work hard at it and you can do well in your life. It's fun to play but at the same time you learn so many life lessons. It helps round you as an individual. That's why I encourage kids to play sports all the time. Those same values that you learn on the court, or on the field, in the ring, or whatever, you have to carry those in your everyday life to be successful.

I think that's why you see that so many athletes in life. You learn that discipline, hard work, that work ethic. You have to know how to carry yourself and deal with adversity for success. It goes along with everyday life. If we don't have enough people out here coaching and teaching these young men and young women about being good citizens and doing well in school and watching over them when they're in the community, they're not going to be any good playing sports or in society.

My first year in Italy, I had an Italian coach who couldn't speak any English. But the way he used to communicate with me was through basketball. By me understanding basketball and growing up playing basketball, I figured basketball was universal. So when he explained something, I was able to catch on. And by me listening to him describe things like shooting drills in Italian, it was helping me learn to speak Italian. The basic principles of understanding basketball came in handle.

The main message that I try to get across to the kids I deal with is that everybody is not going to be a professional basketball player. But that doesn't mean you can't use basketball as a vehicle. That's my thing all the time. Basketball is my vehicle. It teaches you valuable lessons and it can get you places in life. It can afford you the opportunity to go to college for free. It teaches you things that you might not get to learn at home and at school. My message is don't let basketball or any sport use you. You have to use it as a vehicle to get you where you want to go. It might not be the main thing. But it definitely can help you out. There are not enough teams. There are not enough roster spots for every kid in America that wants to play basketball to make it. But you can definitely use basketball to get you to where you want to go.

Scoonie Penn is a personal development coach and camp host who played professionally in Europe for 11 years after a stellar career at Ohio State University. He was drafted by the Atlanta Hawks.

QUOTES

"Success is the result of great habits, tremendous sacrifice, intense preparation, good karma and fearing God. Everything else takes care of itself." William Middlebrooks, head boys basketball coach at Cathedral High School in Los Angeles, CA. He previously coached at Ribet Academy and coached the Compton Magic travel team.

"BIG TEAM little me," Tim Allen, coach Peabody High School in Trenton, Tennessee.

"We are a team. I have to be able to rely on my players and my players have to be able to rely on me." Brad Stevens, Boston Celtics head coach. Before joining the Celtics he was head coach at Butler University.

'Make Tonight Yours' – "A quote from one of our alumni when speaking to our team on senior night. To me, it always means so much when former players come back and speak to our current teams. It means that our program has played a significant role in their lives." Josh Thompson, head boys basketball coach at Bishop McGuinness Catholic High School in Kernersville, NC. He led his team to the 2009 NCHSAA State Championship and is a 3-time Coach of the Year.

"Discipline, unselfishness, and consistency are important factors to a program's success. Discipline allows teams to be efficient with their time and energy. Unselfishness keeps your teams on one central goal and away from personal agendas. Consistency will help you through adversity. All three aspects are critical for a strong program." Brian Robinson, girls head coach at Bishop McGuinness Catholic High School in Kernersville, NC. His team won eight straight girls basketball state championships from 2006-2013. He also was an assistant coach for USA Basketball U16 women's team that won the 2013 gold medal.

"When you have an opportunity to be great, you have to seize the moment. But if you don't seize the moment, you will watch it slip by." Texas Tech men's basketball coach Tubby Smith. He also coached at Minnesota, Tulsa, Georgia, and Kentucky.

"Repetition helps us become successful. So whatever you do over and over, whether it's the right thing or the wrong thing, you will eventually become good at it. I try to get us to do the right things over and over again." Jim Boeheim, head coach of the Syracuse University men's basketball team. He led his team to 29 NCAA appearances and won the national championship in 2003.

"Every time you go to work, you gotta be passionate and positive." Louisville men's head coach and Hall of Famer Rick Pitino, the only coach to win a national championship at two schools, Louisville and Kentucky.

"My role is a coach is to help these young men understand that they are better than they think they are. They are more valuable than they think they are. They are more important than they think they are. And after I do that, then we talk about basketball." Indiana University men's basketball coach Tom Crean, who led Indiana and Marquette teams to the Final Four.

"I think coaching is translated into everything, not just sports.

I have two boys. I'm coaching them. I'm teaching them. It spills over into every area of life." Devean George, three-time NBA champion and 11-year NBA veteran.

"I am big on fundamentals. Once you have your foundation set, you can build from there. Success is about building, one block at a time." Fred Skrocki, who coached the DeJuan Blair-Schenley High School (Pittsburgh, Pa) to the state title in 2007.

"Doing the right things gives you the best chance of winning the game. Doing the wrong things guarantees you that you will lose the game." John Chaney, Hall of Fame Coach and former coach at Temple University.

"We're going to work hard and do all of the things it takes to put us in a position to be successful. If we do that, we'll be all right." Suzie McConnell-Serio, head women's coach at the University of Pittsburgh. Prior to that she coached at Duquesne University and the WNBA's Minnesota Lynx, where she was WNBA Coach of the Year in 2004.

"We're going to use our defense to make us successful." Phil Martelli, head men's coach at Saint Joseph's University.

"You show me a hard worker and I'll show you someone who will get the job done. Hard work and success go hand in hand." Bob Huggins, head men's basketball coach at West Virginia University.

"What do I have to complain about? I get paid to teach basketball and to play a part in the development of young men. Who wouldn't be excited about that job?" Tom Izzo, head men's coach at Michigan State University, where led the team to the 2000 NCAA championship and a trip to the title game in 2009.

OTHER FAMOUS QUOTES

"Be more concerned with your character than your reputation, because your character is what you really are, while your reputation is merely what others think you are." John Wooden, legendary UCLA coach and winner of 10 NCAA championships.

"The strength of the team is each individual member. The strength of each member is the team." Phil Jackson, winner of 11 NBA championship rings as a coach with the Chicago Bulls and Los Angeles Lakers.

"To me, teamwork is the beauty of our sport where you have five acting as one. You become selfless." Mike Krzyzewski, Duke University's men basketball coach and four-time NCAA champion.

"What to do with a mistake – recognize it, admit it, learn from it, forget it." Dean Smith, Hall of Fame coach of the University of North Carolina.

"Show respect for yourself and for your team by working hard and diligently practicing the skills that will give us a good team." Larry Brown, head coach of the men's basketball team at Southern Miss University who has also coached two NBA championship teams.

"Help one kid at a time. He'll maybe go back and help a few more." Al McGuire, who coached Marquette University to the 1977 NCAA championship.

"Systems win! Believe in your system, and then sell it to your players." Billy Donovan, head men's coach at University of Florida, where he won back-to-back NCAA championships in 2006 and 2007.

"All of the successful teams that I've ever seen have three characteristics: They play unselfishly; they play together; and they play hard." Larry Brown, head coach of the men's basketball team at Southern Miss University who has also coached two NBA championship teams.

"Teamwork is really a form of trust. It's what happens when you surrender the mistaken idea that you can go it alone and realize that you won't achieve your individual goals without the support of your colleagues." Pat Summit, former University of Tennessee women's head coach, who won eight NCAA championships.

"Teams that play together beat those teams with superior players who play more as individuals." Jack Ramsey, former NBA coach who led his Portland Trailblazers team to the 1977 NBA championship.

"Successful programs consist of people working hard, working together, while never worrying about who gets the credit." Don Meyer, who finished his coaching career at Northern State University in 2010. He finished with 923 wins and an NAIA national championship.

"Your ability to communicate to your young people will determine your success." Jim Harrick, who led UCLA to a national championship in 1995.

"Good teams become great ones when the members trust each other enough to surrender the Me for the We." Phil Jackson, 11-time NBA champions.

"The key is not the 'will to win' . . . everybody has that. It is the will to prepare to win that is important." Bobby Knight, legendary coach who led Indiana to three NCAA championships in 1976, 1981, and 1987.

"If a coach is determined to stay in the coaching profession, he will develop from year to year. This much is true, no coach has a monopoly on the knowledge of basketball. There are no secrets in the game. The only secrets, if there are any, are good teaching of sound fundamentals, intelligent handling of men, a sound system of play, and the ability to instill in the boys a desire to win." Adolph Rupp, who coached Kansas University for 42 years, including national championships in 1948, 1949, 1951, and 1958.

"Don't give up, don't ever give up." Jim Valvano, who led North Carolina State University to the 1983 NCAA Championship.

AFTERWORDS

Ajamu Banjoko, director of healthy lifestyles, Boys & Girls Clubs of Metro Atlanta

What we want to teach kids at the Boys & Girls Clubs is how to live healthy and what wellness is all about. We have 27 clubs and work with 8,000 kids on a daily basis in Metro Atlanta. We train the staff to be coaches and mentors. The impact the clubs have on kids is phenomenal. A lot of these kids won't have the opportunities to play professional sports. My job is to make sure they're aware of all the options available out there. From a mentoring standpoint whether we directly or indirectly engage young people, we have some type of impact on them.

I had a teen ask me if I was playing. So I laced up my shoes and played some basketball. After the game, I had a chance to talk to him one-on-one. We talked for quite some time. This was positive, meaningful conversation. We had something in common to start the conversation and that was basketball. Then we could talk about things outside of basketball. The mentoring piece was after the fact. We need to make that intentional.

Oftentimes we don't label it as mentoring but *we* see this as a necessity. What we do by coaching and mentoring is help them live a much healthier life. For me, it's an each one, teach one mentality. Kids need positive, strong, dependable and consistent relationships. That's what's missing for a lot of our kids today.

Masud Olufemi, director of healthy lifestyles for the Boys & Girls Clubs of America

Coaching and mentoring has been essential in my personal and professional development. Serving in a movement that promotes leadership and guidance through various programs including athletics, recreation and nutrition education provides me with a great opportunity to help inspire young people and communities to live healthy.

ABOUT THE AUTHOR

C. Nathaniel Brown is a bestselling author, talk show host, motivational and inspirational speaker, and philanthropist. A huge basketball fan, Brown coached middle school and high school basketball in Pittsburgh, Pennsylvania. He founded the Pittsburgh Knights AAU team. He also served as athletic director at Greater Works Academy in Pittsburgh, where he coached girls and later the boys' varsity teams. He began writing about sports for his college newspaper and continued with several newspapers and magazines around the country spanning 21 years. As a writing and publishing coach, he assists writers hone their craft and realize their dreams of publishing. Brown resides in Atlanta, Georgia.

OTHER TITLES

BY C. NATHANIEL BROWN

- ✓ I Always Put the Seat Down
- ✓ Devil in the Mirror: Overcoming the Enemy's Attack
- ✓ Making Wings: Short Stories and Poems
- ✓ The Business of My Book: Make More Money and Reach More People by Understanding the Business of Being a Writer
- ✓ The Hair Commandments: Shalls and Shall Nots of Wigs, Weaves, and Natural Hair (with LaToya Johnson-Rainey)
- ✓ No Timeouts (Coming Winter 2014)

For more information or to order these titles, visit www.EX3ent.com
or
www.CNathanielBrown.net

www.ingramcontent.com/pod-product-compliance
Lightning Source LLC
Chambersburg PA
CBHW071305110426
42743CB00042B/1186